COLLECTOR'S GUIDE TO

Yellow Ware

BOOK III

An Identification & Value Guide

Lisa S.
McAllister

COLLECTOR BOOKS

A Division of Schroeder Publishing Co., Inc.

Front cover, blue and white banded bowl, $100.00 – 135.00; East Liverpool, Ohio signed spaniel, $4,000.00 and up; brown-banded master salt, $475.00 – 650.00; nineteenth century basket, $750.00 and up; unique Cincinnati, Ohio mocha-decorated milk pan with eagle, $6,500.00 and up.

Cover design by Beth Summers
Book design by Heather Warren

COLLECTOR BOOKS
P.O. Box 3009
Paducah, Kentucky 42002-3009

www.collectorbooks.com

Copyright © 2003 Lisa McAllister

The current values in this book should be used only as a guide. They are not intended to set prices, which vary from one section of the country to another. Auction prices as well as dealer prices vary greatly and are affected by condition as well as demand. Neither the author nor the publisher assumes responsibility for any losses that might be incurred as a result of consulting this guide.

Searching For A Publisher?

We are always looking for people knowledgeable within their fields. If you feel that there is a real need for a book on your collectible subject and have a large comprehensive collection, contact Collector Books.

Contents

Dedication

I met Byron Dillow and his wife, Sara, early on in my career. From the beginning, they trusted my judgment and intuition in helping to build their yellow ware collection. We learned together on many occasions. Byron passed away on September 12, 2002. He was a family man and a friend who helped us out in areas that he was knowledgeable in. Sara, along with Byron, helped to shape what yellow ware collecting is today. Sara offered the following comment on Byron, "...One of his favorite things was to have the table set with yellow ware pie plates and serving bowls – he enjoyed using the pieces as well as displaying them and visiting with people about the collection." He is greatly missed.

Acknowledgments

To my husband, Barry McAllister, who keeps going, despite all.

A big THANK YOU to everyone who helped me. If I have forgotten to thank you in print, I am sorry, let me know!

Amy Sullivan and Gail Ashburn of Collector Books

Firstlook Photo, Hagerstown, Maryland and their friendly, knowledgeable staff

Susan Airey
Karen Allen
Beaver Creek Antique Market, Hagerstown, Maryland
Warren Broderick, who generously provided information and photos of his collection
Arthur Goldberg
Gene Haney
Dayna Harple
Joan Jeffrey
Joanne Kennedy
Deborah Lemieux
Bill Lewan
Al Marzorini
Mears and Boyer
Barbara and Fran Riggs
Ann Sahlman, who generously photographed her collection of bowls
Maryann Stolar
J. Garrison Stradling
Wayne and Rosemary Van Derzell

Ten years ago I started writing about yellow ware, and it is still exciting for me today. There seem to be a limitless number of forms, decorations and experimental changes to see, like a Rebekah at the Well teapot with blue glaze, or a Jeffords basketweave teapot with a pour spout instead of a gooseneck spout. Many people are surprised to hear that there is enough new/fresh yellow ware and information to fill a third book. You be the judge, but I think that you will find this third book as informative as the first two books. I've been collecting photographs of yellow ware that I have bought for the last five plus years, and also photos from my customers, in preparation for this book. There are more than 300 photos that run the gamut from twentieth century banded bowls to wonderful animals to rare marks on yellow ware.

You will note in all three books that prices have risen, in most cases. In the 20 years I've been in the antique business, this is the general rule on pieces that are scarce or rare. Collectors have groaned about the prices of mocha-decorated yellow ware, for example, as long as I've been a dealer, but it has never gone down in price. I learned quickly that if it is a piece you rarely see, mocha or not, you should step up and buy it. (Of course there are situations where price is a factor, but if you read these books, you will be prepared.) This lesson has served not only myself, but many collectors as well. Beware of a huge price jump in pieces that are frequent in every antique mall and show. The escalation of the price on a common item is due to hype and popularity, not value. When this happens, prices will eventually fall, sometimes dramatically. Getting good value for your money does not necessarily mean buying something for nothing, but that what you buy at least *holds* its value, and, under the best circumstances, rises over time. Auctions are not usually a good way to judge accurate prices. Two

identical pieces of yellow ware can sell for $20.00 or $1,000.00, depending on conditions. Is the item accurately described? The above prices were paid, within days, for two identical items at two different auctions. The seller who got $20.00 for his piece described it accurately as a French yellow earthenware mold dipped in brown glaze and having some multicolored slip decoration. The seller who got $1,000.00 described his mold as a rare mocha-decorated yellow ware mold, which does not exist. Another condition that is frequent at auctions is that bidders bid "just so the other guy won't get it," or feelings to that effect. It is impossible to gauge an accurate price in this situation.

A word about condition. I have learned, through experience and from others, that the rarer a piece is, the more damage it can have and still be acceptable. This is not something that I created, but a reality in collecting antiques. Museums (and serious collectors) abound with great pieces that are in used condition. When the lure is perfection over quality, you can set yourself up to unknowingly buy a new or repaired piece. If you don't want to be fooled by new or repaired pieces, my suggestion is that you own one or more pieces of each. The sooner you can spot a new piece, or a restoration, the less money you will lose. Restored pieces of yellow ware are acceptable and unavoidable, but you have to weigh the rarity of the piece against the price. Experience is the best teacher.

I have been asked questions involving learning about yellow ware and how to tell if a piece is old or valuable. The above advice about buying new and repaired pieces is one way to learn. The best way to learn (and the quickest and least expensive) is nothing more than owning real yellow ware and studying it. The "real yellow ware" means that the pieces are nineteenth century, not 1930s mixing bowls or casserole dishes. The studying part is living with the piece every day, comparing it to similar pieces at antiques shows and auctions, and reading all books on the subject (not just mine!). When you know what real yellow ware looks like and feels like, you will have a much easier time buying it. This is how I learned. When I want to learn about something new to me, I buy a few authentic pieces and books to study on that subject. I'm always surprised when people educate themselves for a job, but think that collecting antiques needs no education. Unless you just want a shelf of yellow pottery, education pays.

In some descriptions I have not listed sizes. There are instances where this is not a factor in the valuation of an item.

My introduction in Book 2 sums up how I still feel about yellow ware five years later. It is interesting, regardless of your desire. You can get it plain or fancy, decorative or useful. Buying, selling, sharing, and studying yellow ware has been a wonderful life experience for me. I've met so many people who in their own way have expanded my life. I look forward to doing this for many years.

If you would like to purchase yellow ware or want information, please contact Lisa McAllister by phone at 301-842-3255 or e-mail at www.mcallisterinc.com.

Lisa S. McAllister

This section on marks illustrates the actual marks, instead of a printed list of potters. Since most yellow ware is unmarked, you could search in vain for many potters' marks. Shown here are marks you could find. I would highly recommend purchasing Lois Lehner's *Encyclopedia of U.S. Marks on Pottery, Porcelain, and Clay*, and Geoffrey A. Godden's *Encyclopedia of British Pottery and Porcelain Marks*. Both of these books illustrate the shape of a mark, thereby making it easier for you to define an actual mark.

Rockingham and pewter teapot: Thomas Smith of Boston, Massachusetts, patented this teapot on Oct. 4, 1870. His patent number is 108,061.

Bowl and pitcher embossed with daisies: "WOOD," England, 1820 – 1830.

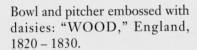

Octagonal teapot with Oriental figures: William Schreiber of Phoenixville, Pennsylvania held the patent for this teapot. Phoenixville was a busy pottery center, the largest potter being Griffin, Smith, and Hill. The major output for G., S., & H. was majolica, for which yellow ware was the body in many cases. It pays to look on the bottom of yellow ware pieces, even ones you are not interested in, because you may find a good mark like this patent date.

Spittoon: Beneath the swan is impressed, "HANKS & FISH SWAN HILL POTTERY S. AMBOY., N.J.," circa 1849 – 1876. The Swan Hill Pottery included a number of potters: created by Charles Fish; later owned by a son-in-law, Harry Clay Perrine; James Carr and Thomas Locker; and John L. Rue.

Flower frog: The Weller Pottery started production in 1872, when Samuel A. Weller went into business doing what he had done since a boy. The pottery started in Fultonham, near Zanesville, and eventually moved to Zanesville. Although Weller made art pottery as well, is made quite a bit of kitchen ware, especially in the 1930s. The pieces that yellow ware collectors are most familiar with are the brown-banded mixing bowls and other pieces in that line: batter bowls (Book 1), custard cups, graduated pitchers, etc. The mark shown is also on the kitchen wares and dates circa 1920 – 1930. The base of the flower frog is unglazed. Many of the banded pieces are unglazed as well on the base.

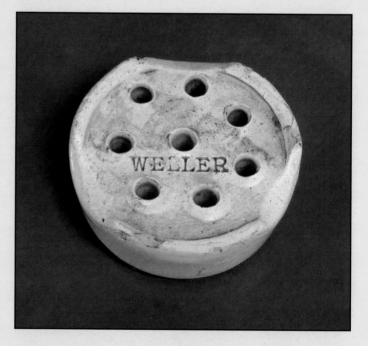

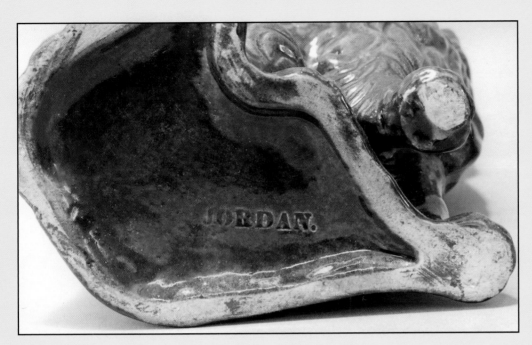

Pair of Rockingham spaniels: "JORDAN." is a town in New York, near Syracuse. From circa 1827 to 1856, there were a variety of potters at work. Sidney N. Norton, James McBurney and his three sons, and Franklin L. Sheldon, all potted in Jordan. Since the style of spaniels is about 1850 – 1860, they were produced late in Jordan's pottery history.

"WARRANTED SHARPE'S FIRE PROOF." Thomas Sharpe and Brothers, circa 1821 – 1895, making earthenware and stoneware. Their primary product was utilitarian yellow ware and later added Rockingham. Yellow ware was also called Derbyshire Ironstone, or Derbyshire Cane Ware, because there was so much yellow ware produced in Derbyshire, England.

Platter: Uriah Kendall and his son made pottery in Cincinnati from about 1840 to 1850. They produced yellow ware, Rockingham, and stoneware.

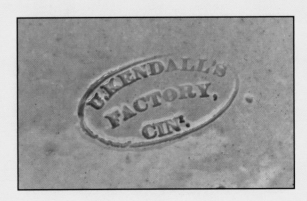

Black scenic transfer mug: "J. THOMPSON HARTSHORNE POTTERY NEAR ASHBY DE LE ZOUCH." Joseph Thompson, Derbyshire, England, from circa 1818 to 1882. This printed mark dates circa 1840 – 1856. The later marks were impressed "J.THOMPSON" or "JOSEPH THOMPSON/WOODEN BOX/POTTERY/DERBYSHIRE."

Jumbo the Elephant: "THE GLOBE POTTERY EAST LIVERPOOL, O." with a globe in a circle. A short-lived mark, 1888 – 1901. Globe Pottery originated as Frederick, Shenkle, Allen Co., and merged with East Liverpool Potteries Co., in 1901. Globe Pottery opened again in 1907, but did not produce yellow ware. Globe was known for its figural pieces.

Individual oval dish: W. H. Grindley and Co., Ltd., Tunstall, Staffordshire, England. Although the company started about 1880, this printed mark is from 1954 to 1960. There are some yellow pieces that have this consistency of potting, a refined, smooth mix of earthenware and stoneware with a semi-clear, high gloss. They have an opaque appearance, and you cannot "see" past the glaze, as you can with earlier yellow ware. I have had this piece for a few years to study and compare to many other yellow pieces. Yellow ware ladles appear to be made by Grindley. The name "PETAL WARE," I am assuming, refers to flower petals of yellow, the same way Dandy Line refers to dandelions.

Pear-shaped snuff jar: "BERLIN SNUFF HENRY ARND BALTI-MORE" is a vendor's mark. This is a wonderful mark, with the name and place of the vendor inside an embossed medallion in the shape of the jar. The center of the mark is a phoenix and shield.

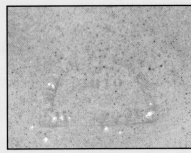

Plate with curved sides: "CROXALL AND BROS EAST LIVERPOOL OHIO" in a semi-circle, circa 1888 – 1914. The Croxall family was a major producer of yellow ware and Rockingham in East Liverpool prior to 1888.

Pineapple pitcher: "W & J.A. BAILEY PAT APPLE (?) ALLOA." Scotland, 1855 – 1908. This mark is probably 1855 – 1890, since this pottery produced majolica, in which yellow ware could be used as the body. The company also produced a high quantity of Rockingham.

Plain yellow presentation pitcher: "CHS COXON STH AMBOY NJ," 1858 – 1860. Prior to running Swan Hill, Coxon worked for Edwin Bennett in Baltimore. Among his achievements in Baltimore was the Rebekah at the Well teapot, the Toby mug and the covered pitcher with herons. The Toby mugs from both Bennett and Swan Hill are attributed to Coxon. After Swan Hill, he was in Trenton and secured enough money by 1863 to start his own pottery. In partnership with John S. Thompson, they produced their version of creamware, and white graniteware. Coxon's Ellsworth pitcher in white graniteware was his highest achievement in the seven years he potted in Trenton. He died in 1868, having left a wealth of great designs.

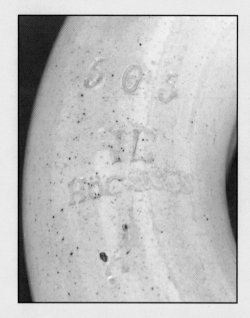

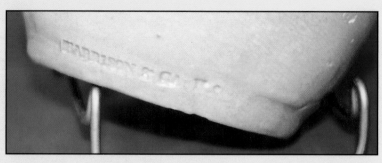

Bottle: The mark of Harrison & Cash is a vendor's mark, since there is no known pottery by this name. Both bottles with this mark were found in New Hampshire.

Ring mold: "HOGANAS." Sweden, circa 1840 – 1870. This yellow ware is finely made, very smooth and with few impurities. Many times these pieces are dark golden yellow, even pumpkin colored. Molds of unusual design are usually found, although there are jars, mugs, etc. Along with the Hoganas name, there may be numbers or letters. These allow us to date the piece and sometimes identify the potter.

(Below) Two pitchers and a toothbrush holder: Three marks of the T.G. Green & Co., Church Gresley, near Burton-on-Trent (Derbyshire), England, from 1864 to at least 2003. This company makes earthenware and stoneware. One of its most famous products is Cornish Ware, a kitchen line made of white-bodied stoneware with wide blue, yellow, or red bands. The yellow ware version of Cornish Ware has white bands and is called Cornish Gold. All of the Green pieces have value, but you do have to keep age in mind when purchasing.

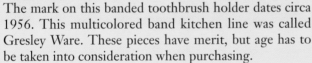

This mark is on the large pear-shaped jug that can be found with a matching basin (T.G. Green sold them separately). The bands are narrow black or brown, and very wide white, circa 1930 – 1960.

The mark on this banded toothbrush holder dates circa 1956. This multicolored band kitchen line was called Gresley Ware. These pieces have merit, but age has to be taken into consideration when purchasing.

This circular Green mark was used on yellow ware circa 1900 – 1930. The mark shown is on a mocha-decorated pitcher that has blue and brown scenic seaweed. An important fact: Green made some of best seaweed-mocha pieces you will find. The company made single and bi-colored pitchers, bowls, chambers, etc. with green, brown, blue, and/or red seaweed. Green is the only producer of mocha pieces of this vintage that used red seaweed. The seaweed is usually very well-defined. However, you should know that you are buying a piece that is most likely from the twentieth century, not the nineteenth century. There can be a *big* difference in value.

Banded rolling pins have continued to be almost impossible to find. Although this is a different band pattern than the rolling pin in Book 1, Brush McCoy made both from 1915 to 1925. Depending on price, this piece is worth purchasing in any condition. $2,000.00 and up.

This miniature bowl and pitcher set dates about 1830 – 1840 and is English. As small as it is, the applied floral decoration still has great detail. $1,250.00 – 1,500.00.

Although this piece looks like a miniature funnel, it fits into the rim of a mug to be used for shaving. Third quarter nineteenth century, United States or England. $135.00 – 165.00.

Most meat tenderizers are stoneware, which makes sense because of the hard use intended. This one is yellow ware with a white glaze. Don't confuse yellow stoneware examples, usually with a Christmas patent date of 1877, with lighter weight yellow ware examples. $450.00 – 550.00.

A shaped, concave rim sets off this miniature/toy vegetable dish. Nineteenth century United States or England. $200.00 – 250.00.

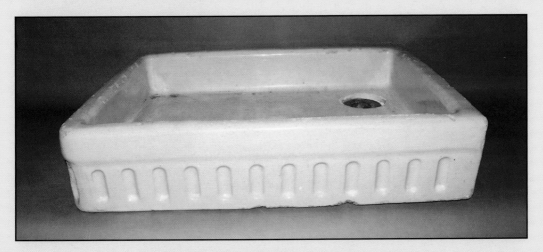

Although there is a high percentage of stoneware in this sink, it is truly yellow ware. A novel use for the versatile yellow clay. United States. $500.00 and up.

This 4" tall American piece is a stove foot. Since these were something that got hard use, stove feet were more often produced using stoneware. There were not many made due to their impractical nature. Third quarter nineteenth century. $225.00 – 295.00.

Right: This majestic water cooler and stand has an interesting blue/brown/white slip glaze. Painted over the glaze in black letters is "Thomas Radium CR Patented 7 16 12 other patents p'dg." Ohio. $2,000.00 and up.

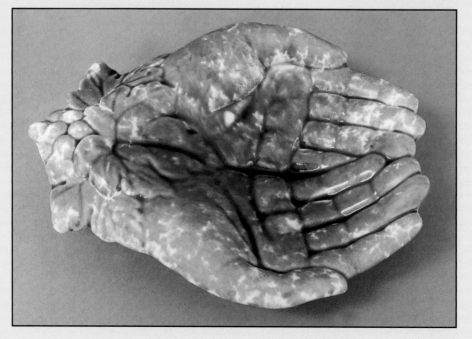

This dish, shaped like a pair of outstretched hands, is identical in form to one made in graniteware at the Bennington pottery, 1850 – 1858. (Graniteware is similar to white ironstone in density and coloring.) Since the pottery at Bennington was known to make Rockingham-decorated yellow ware, this is one way to attribute pieces. 7" long. $500.00 and up.

This great Rockingham-decorated inkwell was produced at Bennington, Vermont, 1853 – 1858. The shaped "dome" held quite a bit of ink and made the inkwell easy to fit in the hand. Look closely at the top of the base and you will see the hole for the pen. There is a fill hole on the bottom of the inkwell that, when turned upright, did not need a cork, through some type of capillary action the ink remained in the well without spilling. 4" high. $500.00 and up.

The black and pinky-mauve slip decoration on this bank are the distinctive colors used in Yorkshire, England on many yellow ware pieces. 4½" tall, circa 1810. $750.00 – 895.00.

Miniature Rockingham-decorated keeler, United States, third quarter nineteenth century. $350.00 – 450.00.

The density and lack of contrast in the Rockingham application on this large urn suggests that it is of Ohio manufacture, possibly Cincinnati. A rare form with the pewter spigot still in place. 1850 – 1880. $2,000.00 and up.

Rockingham-decorated cradles, produced in England, circa 1820, were made as christening gifts. The addition of blue seaweed mocha on white slip, however, makes this cradle unique at this time. $2,500.00 and up.

Toy tea services that are dated this early are not usually found. The Adam Buck-style transfers help to date the pieces to the 1820s. He was an Irish miniaturist who worked in London. Note that the tea set has brick red striping that matches the transfers, and that the cup and saucer have green striping. The scale is slightly larger as well on the green-edged cup and saucer. Other toy pieces have been found with this type of transfer. Set of teapot, sugar bowl, cream pitcher: $695.00 – 895.00. Cup and saucer: $125.00 – 185.00.

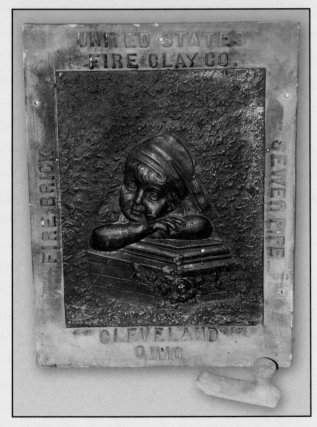

I could find no information about this company, "UNITED STATES FIRE CLAY CO. CLEVELAND OHIO." Fire clay was another name for yellow ware. Only a few pottery wall placques are known, surely because they had no protection from the elements. This piece is a good example of unglazed yellow ware. It would have been brighter when first produced, but since it was not glazed it has had no protection from dirt and grime. A bronze slip was painted over the molded design of the girl. Late 1800s. $1,500.00 and up.

The form and decoration help to date this spill vase to circa 1830, England. A spill is a slender piece of wood or twisted paper used to light a candle or lamp, for example. It is the precursor to matches. The multicolored flowers and oxblood striping are painted over the glaze, so they have no protection from wear. This particular decoration was used on other English ceramics with the same form. 5" high. $550.00 – 650.00.

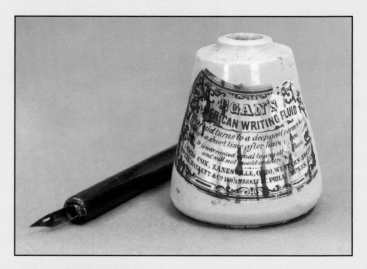

What a find, to have the paper advertising label on this inkwell. It advertises Egan's American writing fluid, and lists the Eastern agent (Philadelphia) and the Western agent (Zanesville, Ohio). Most likely made in Ohio, mid to late 1800s. $450.00 – 550.00.

Although resembling a candle-holder, this is a match safe. The striker is the unglazed, coggled base. United States, 1850 – 1880. $185.00 – 275.00.

Rarely seen forms, scoops were easily broken. This example is about 5" long and was probably produced in Europe, circa 1900. $450.00. – 550.00.

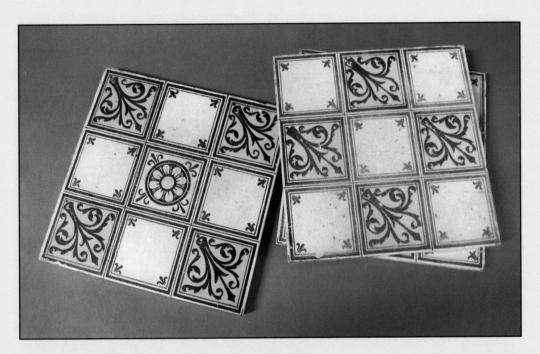

Yellow ware tiles were produced in England about the third quarter of the nineteenth century. They contain some stoneware in the body, due to their practical usage. The method of decoration is transfer printing and ranged from geometric to bucolic in nature. The colors used here are brown, and black. Average size is about 5" square. $120.00 – 250.00 each.

This large, rectangular piece is a downspout, produced in Ohio, possibly Cincinnati, circa 1870. This clay would have a mix of yellow ware and stoneware for strength. Unique at this time. $550.00 – 650.00.

Ashtrays are another rare use of yellow ware. The octagonal form has refined clay, a white slip lining, and is marked "Cobridge 1938 B." An interesting feature is the angled hole in the rear to allow it to hang on a wall. England. $150.00 – 225.00.

These candlesticks have flint enamel glaze and great form. The deep, openwork bases are 4½" in diameter; overall height 9¼" high. Attributed to the Trenton, New Jersey area, circa 1860. For the pair, $2,250.00 and up.

Egg cup with black seaweed on a dark orange slip band, accented by narrow white slip bands. Most egg cups are about 2½" high. England, 1850 – 1880. $650.00 – 750.00

Both of these toy potties have great mocha decoration. On the left, bi-colored blue and brown seaweed each on a different slip band. circa 1900, England. $900.00 and up. On the right, a combed slip design. United States or England, circa 1890. $350.00 – 450.00.

Although these pieces are shaped like egg cups, they are almost too small for that purpose. They may have been cordial cups. The Rockingham decoration is fairly solid, with gilded bands. England or Europe, circa 1880. $150.00 – 225.00 each.

An umbrella stand produced by the Robinson-Ransbottom Pottery in Roseville, Ohio, circa 1925. The origin of this company was Whitmore, Robinson and Company, 1862 – 1900. This pottery made yellow ware and Rockingham among other ceramics. After various mergers between 1900 and 1920, the pottery became Robinson-Ransbottom and is still in business today. The umbrella stand is 22" tall and has cobalt blue dripped glaze. The applied and scrolled shell handles have Rockingham glaze. A rare form. $895.00 and up.

Rockingham decoration is rarely found on chamber pots, regardless of size. This is a toy example. Ohio, east to Maryland and New York. $295.00 – 375.00.

Yellow ware bird whistles, made as toys for children, are in short supply. John Henderson, a potter in East Liverpool, Ohio, circa 1847 – 1857, was a maker of bird whistles and toys. 4" long, 3" high. $495.00 – 595.00.

As shown in this chapter, footwarmers are generally long, somewhat tubular containers, with openings at the top for hot water and handles on the sides. The exception to this rule is the solid, brick-shaped form, whose stamp on the bottom leaves no doubt as to its use. The handles on the plain yellow examples are identical to finials used on pipkin lids, for pipkins marked "YELLOW ROCK PHILA" or "J.E. JEFFORDS PHILA." Embossed designs and colored glazes were also used. United States, 1850 – 1890. Average length, 12" to 14". Expect damage due to the nature of their use. $300.00 – 500.00 each.

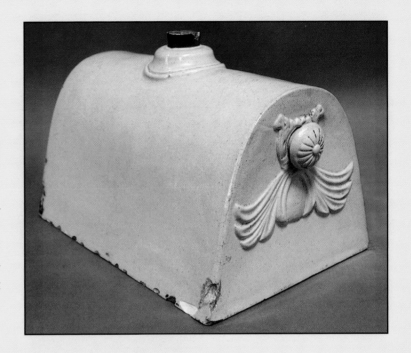

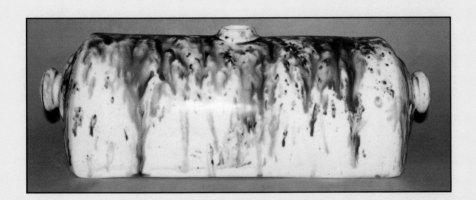

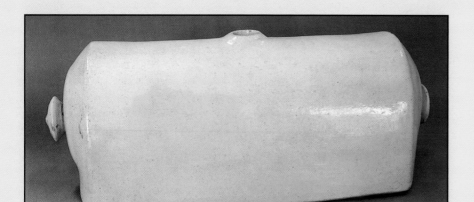

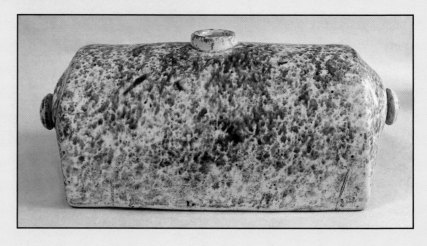

Embossed teapots are usually plain but this example has colored slip and gilding as well. Perhaps more teapots like this one were made at the factory, but the decoration wore off. United States, circa 1880. $450.00 – 550.00.

This tall, plain, yellow coffee pot looks somewhat modern, but dates circa 1880. A unique form in yellow ware at this time. United States. $1,250.00 and up.

Banded teapot with nine narrow blue and white slip bands on base and lid. This pattern of bands must have been popular since it is found on mustard pots, mugs, and pitchers, among other forms. England, 1840 – 1860. $1,750.00 and up.

Tea and Coffee Pots

This highly crafted English teapot exhibits a wide range of potters' skills. It has engine turning, rouletted bands, and pink lustre decoration. The flowers are enameled (painted), and the bird spout and handle are wonderful. This was a very expensive piece to produce. Circa 1840. $750.00 – 850.00.

Engine-turning and rouletted bands set this banded teapot apart from other banded teapots. These features, along with the acanthus leaf decoration on the spout, help to date this piece to circa 1820. This is a larger example as well. England. $2,500.00 and up.

Rockingham-decorated coffeepot, marked "J.B Patterson, Fire-Clay Ware Manufactory, Pottsville, PA." Although of nineteenth century manufacture, no exact dates are known for this pottery. To date, most pieces found from this factory are flat forms; pie plates, and nappies. The hollow forms found are a few molds, waste bowls, and this coffeepot. $1,500.00 and up.

William Schreiber was the maker of this stylish Rockingham teapot. The basic form is identical to most Rebekah style teapots, but the Oriental figures design is rare. Schreiber's patented base design is corrugated for the escape of hot air. This kept the contents from burning, and the teapot from cracking or bursting. (See Potters' marks for a photo of this patent date.) $450.00 – 550.00.

The Rebekah at the Well teapot is the most common form of yellow ware produced, other than the twentieth century mixing bowl. The teapots were made at so many different potteries that it is difficult to know the maker, since almost all are unmarked. The inspiration for the design on the teapot fits the story of Rebekah from the Bible, but that is not the reason for the popularity of this teapot.

The Independent Order of Odd Fellows created the Rebekah Degree in 1851. Its headquarters were in Baltimore, Maryland, home of the E. and W. Bennett pottery. Edwin started the pottery in 1846 and was joined by William in 1847. The Rebekah Degree allowed women related to an I.O.O.F. member to join the Daughters of Rebekah. These teapots must have been very much in demand for all of the social functions of the Daughters of Rebekah. Also, many potters in the United States were members of the I.O.O.F., which may be equally as important a factor in their popularity. Regardless of the reason, this is the most successful teapot design ever produced.

It is most likely that the Bennett pottery was the first maker of Rebekah teapots. Marked Rebekah sugar bowls by this pottery are known to exist. Charles Coxon was the designer of Bennett's Rebekah teapot. He left in 1858 after eight years in Baltimore to run the Swan Hill pottery. The decoration on these pieces may have been applied, in layers in some cases, rather than molded, and an examination of various Rebekah teapots will substantiate this process. The Rebekah design is thought to have come from a pitcher with a similar design, produced by Samuel Alcock in the 1840s.

Due to improvements in the design of the base, most Rebekah teapots found today were produced after 1870. There is a tremendous variance in shape, size, and design. Sizes range from about one cup to just over one gallon. Glazes can be solid or variegated. Many Rebekah teapots are plain; some have extraordinary details. On some Rebekah teapots, there is no name; on others, the name may be Anglicized to Rebecca. Depending on the factors listed, you could buy a Rebekah at the Well teapot for as little as $50.00, or well into the hundreds.

Potters experimented with ornamentation and practicality by using metal appendages on pottery pieces. This teapot has an ornate spout, lid, and handle in pewter. This is a fine marriage of two different arts. Marked "T.Smith/Ptd. Oct. 4, 1870," Boston, Massachusetts, 7" tall. $550.00 – 650.00.

The large size of this coffeepot allowed the potter plenty of area for a great scenic pink lustre design. Decorated on both sides and on the lid. England, circa 1830. $1,000.00 and up.

A rare blue-glazed cylindrical teapot, possibly Ohio, circa 1880. It has "Merry Christmas" etched on one side and "Happy New Year" etched on the other side. With lid, $550.00 – 650.00.

The Cartwright Brothers pottery in East Liverpool, Ohio sold an identical teapot with a wire handle as a tilting kettle. It sat in a metal frame so you would not have to touch the hot teapot. Also, the space between the base of the frame and the teapot allowed air to circulate and keep the teapot from cracking. The chunky teapot with the pottery handle may have been made as an alternative. There was obvious experimentation with glazes and designs. Other East Liverpool potteries may have made this design as well as Cartwright. Circa 1880. Rockingham teapots, $395.00 – 495.00. Blue-glazed teapot, $500.00 and up.

An unusual form for a yellow ware plate, a shallow, rounded form with a coggled rim. This style of plate is most often produced in redware. Make sure you are buying yellow ware, not redware with a yellow glaze. Possibly Pennsylvania, mid to late 1800s. $225.00 – 295.00.

A thinly potted, shallow plate, with a low relief embossed design on the verge. Possibly a soup plate, late nineteenth century. United States or England. $250.00 – 325.00.

Wedgwood produced this yellow ware plate, with its shallow but heavily detailed design, with majolica (green) glazes as well. Yellow ware was used frequently as a base, or blank, for majolica pieces. $100.00 – 125.00.

Plain yellow platters are rare; this example is marked "U. KENDALL'S FACTORY, CIN. O." Uriah Kendall and his son produced yellow ware, Rockingham and stoneware, from about 1840 to 1850, in Cincinnati, Ohio. (See Potters' Marks to see this mark.) $1,000.00 and up.

Two English cake plates, showing embossed designs of people and flowers, 9" in diameter each, 1850 to 1880. Each, $375.00 – 495.00.

This oval platter is French and is true yellow ware, not the pale earthenware sometimes found produced in France as well. Marked "APT," a pottery that started in 1750, producing wares other than yellow ware. The value is lower than the Kendall platter, due to the demand for American yellow ware over European yellow ware in this country. 1850 – 1880. $375.00 – 495.00.

East Liverpool, Ohio platters with Rockingham decoration. Note the shallow embossed designs around the rims. Mid to late 1800s. $395.00 – 595.00 each, depending on size.

A thickly potted saucer (?), with a debossed design of scrolling and potted flowers, nineteenth century. $225.00 – 295.00.

This advertising pie plate, for a confectioner (bakery) in Albany, New York, is unique at this time. It was made in England and is marked "SHARPE'S WARRANTED FIREPROOF," 1821 – 1895. $450.00 – 550.00.

Plate with curved sides, marked "CROXALL AND BROS EAST LIVERPOOL OHIO." Note that the clay is darker on the bottom half of the plate. This bi-colored clay can also be found on nappies and pie plates made in the United States and England. (See Potters' Marks for this mark). $450.00 – 550.00.

Food molds have been in use for thousands of years. Egyptian hieroglyphics show bakers using molds to bake bread into the shape of animals. Early forms, circa 79, include shells, rabbits and pigs. Romans molded food into the shapes of fish, hens, and doves. Gelatin made from animal feet and bones was used in molds prior to the invention of packaged gelatin. This was a time-consuming procedure. Two ingredients were used in the 1800s as thickeners: a variety of seaweed called Irish Moss, and cornstarch. The latter was patented in 1840, and spurred the making of blank mange, a sweet pudding that was made with milk, vanilla, and sometimes rum or kirsch. For more information on molds, please refer to Books 1 and 2.

Cherub holding a bird. United States or England, 1850 – 1870. $500.00 and up.

Rockingham-decorated mold showing a peacock, rare subject matter for a yellow ware mold. Nineteenth century, England. $500.00 and up.

Farmer milking a cow. Mainly found in pearl-ware or white ironstone, so it is English, 1840 – 1860. $500.00 and up.

This huge mold, showing a pear and leaves with a grape cluster, is marked "HOGANAS." The exterior walls and shaped base would facilitate handling. Part of the value here is in the size of this mold. Sweden, 1850 – 1865. $595.00 – 795.00.

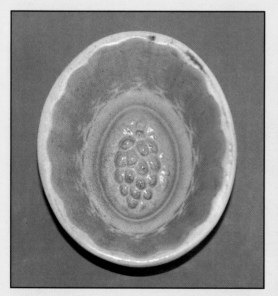

A deep mold, showing a cluster of grapes surrounded by leaves. United States, 1860 – 1900. $185.00 – 250.00.

A nappy is the form for this mold showing a cluster of tulips. A tulip petal is the design for the perimeter of the mold. Also found with a Rockingham glaze. United States, probably Ohio, third quarter nineteenth century. $350.00 – 450.00.

 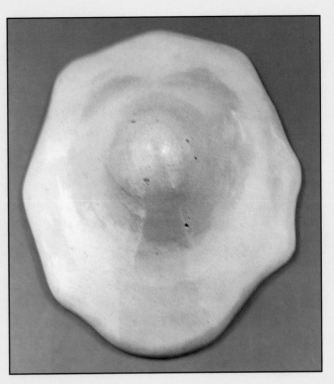

Although this mold is thickly potted, the base indicates an earlier date of manufacture than many other yellow ware molds. The earliest molds, made of creamware, have no rim or feet but an uneven bottom, caused by resting in sand while the mold hardened. The lion is a popular motif in English ceramics. This mold would have been used in a hotel or very large home. Length – 9", width – 7¼", circa 1840 – 1850. $1,000.00 and up.

 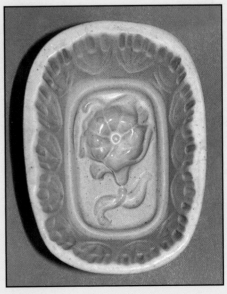

A deep rectangular mold, measuring 4½" long, showing two fat pieces of fruit between a cluster of leaves. United States or England, mid-nineteenth century. $325.00 – 395.00.

Flower or blossom with highly detailed walls. United States or England, mid-nineteenth century. $500.00 and up.

Ring mold, 8½" by 2½" deep. An uncommon form. Hoganas, Sweden, 1850s to 1860s. $295.00 – 395.00.

Round mold showing a dogwood blossom, with a pointed leaf design on the side walls. Approximately 7" diameter. United States or England, nineteenth century. $395.00 – 595.00.

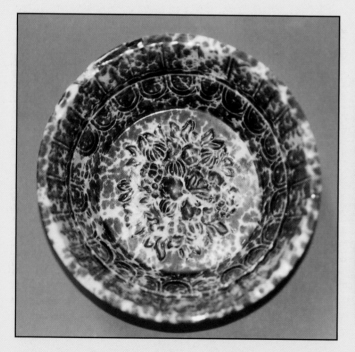

Rockingham-decorated mold showing a cluster of fruit and leaves. The brown glaze tends to obscure the small design. United States or England, 1850 – 1880. $395.00 – 495.00.

Big sunflower mold, 7½" diameter. Great design. England, nineteenth century. $500.00 and up.

This is number 16 of the Yellow Rock mini-molds, also shown in Books 1 (two molds) and 2 (13 molds). Although this one is similar to a few other mini-molds, it is not identical. $195.00 – 250.00.

Small oval mold with a turtle. This mold is nearly impossible to find. United States or England, nineteenth century. $750.00 and up.

Cluster of fruit, with net or scale-like sides. 6" long. United States, late 1800s. $295.00 – 395.00.

This is an unusual example of the wheat mold. The blue and brown scroddled slip makes it unique. Scroddling is a vein-like design that can be either part of the glaze or in the clay. United States, 1860 – 1880. $395.00 – 495.00.

"Cornish Ware" covered soap dish with removable drainer. This band pattern was used on an earlier line of T.G. Green yellow ware, up to the 1930s. Again, a full line of kitchen and toilet pieces was produced. $225.00 – 300.00.

Toothbrush holder with distinctive black, brown, and blue bands, representative of the Gresley Ware line. The clay used for these pieces was very refined and "hard," with a high percentage of stoneware. A full line of kitchen and toilet pieces was produced, circa 1956, T.G. Green & Co., Ltd., Church Gresley, England. $165.00 – 225.00.

This beautifully embossed pitcher and bowl set is marked "WOOD" and was produced in England 1820 – 1830. Since there were various potters by this name, it is impossible to make a firm attribution. Children's plates of this era can be found with the identical daisy embossing on their borders. $1,850.00 and up.

Unique at this time, a yellow ware urinal with Rockingham decoration. United States or Canada, third quarter nineteenth century. Many chamber pots were dropped, accidentally or not, into the outhouse while emptying them. I would imagine that there are fair numbers of these urinals in the same place. $150.00 – 250.00.

Nearly all yellow ware soap dishes are one piece; this example has a removable drainer. A primitive piece with tiny, impractical holes in the drainer, this may have been an experimental piece. United States, nineteenth century. $495.00 – 595.00.

An unusual octagonal spittoon, with a strong visual pattern in the Rockingham and green oxide glaze. United States, 1860 – 1900. $295.00 – 395.00.

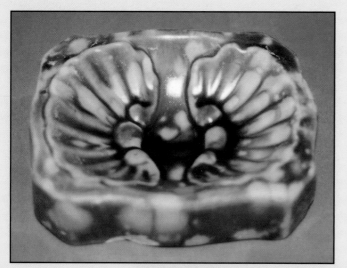

This Rockingham-decorated soap dish, with its embossed shell design, may reflect the proximity of its maker to the Atlantic Ocean. It is attributed to the Bennett pottery in Baltimore, Maryland, circa 1850 – 1856. $200.00 – 275.00.

An unusual plain chamber pot, since most are decorated in some fashion. Third quarter nineteenth century, United States. $250.00 – 350.00.

Almost 7" long, this elliptical soap dish has a lot of embossed detail. Most plain yellow soap dishes have no molded designs. Produced for a large home or hotel. United States, 1850 – 1900. $550.00 – 650.00.

This unique spittoon dates circa 1820 because of the rouletted bands on top, middle and bottom. The blue seaweed design is finely done as a flower and ferns. An incredible piece of workmanship. The tiny strap handle would accommodate one finger. England or Scotland. $2,500.00 and up.

Yellow ware chamber pots were obviously a great canvas for mocha decoration. Not a dull one in the group! The green dot-seaweed design is unique in its color and pattern, and both it and the blue floral seaweed chamber pots are English or Scottish. The Oyster slip mocha design was produced in Baltimore Maryland. 1840 – 1870. Each, $950.00 and up.

A great Rockingham-decorated spittoon with an historical motif. Lady Liberty stands as a column separating clusters of stars. The flared rope-embossed rim is easy to pick up and hold. Jersey City Pottery Co., circa 1865 – 1885. 8" diameter. $450.00 – 550.00.

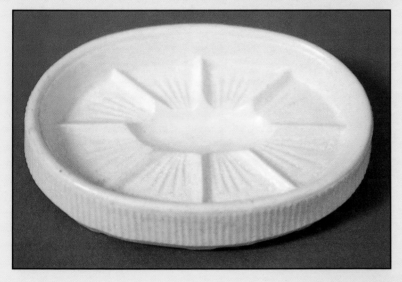

This is an interesting one-piece soap dish, only 1" deep. The design is attractive and functional. It has pad feet on the base similar to a nappy and is hollow. United States, 1850 – 1900. $400.00 – 495.00.

Yellow ware that is sponged or dipped in cobalt blue glaze is not common. The embossed design on this spittoon has a cameo-like medallion in the center and is embossed on both sides. This type of design is attributed to either the Swan Hill Pottery or J.E. Jeffords, Philadelphia, Pennsylvania, circa 1870. 8" in diameter. $450.00 – 550.00.

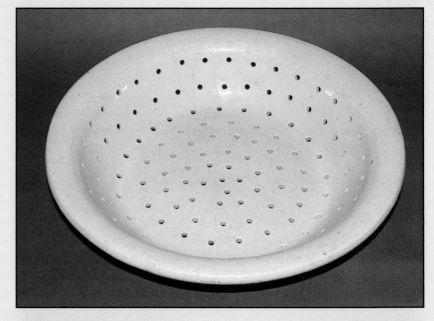

French, basin-shaped colander with peg feet, 1850 – 1880. This colander can also be found with Rockingham decoration in large splotches. Very practical for its intended use since the holes are all the way up to the rim. 11½" in diameter, 1¾" deep. $450.00 – 575.00.

The bold blue and white band pattern on this colander can also be found on pitchers and crocks. Connecting band patterns on different forms is one way to determine the maker or origin of yellow ware pieces. $1,450.00 and up.

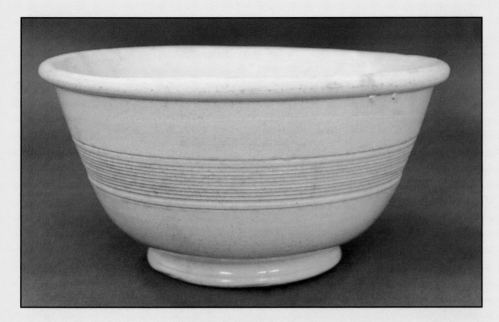

The engine-turned band helps to date this small, plain colander. The circa 1850 date of manufacture makes this piece one of the later engine-turned pieces. English. $450.00 – 575.00.

The brown and white band pattern shown here is identical to that used on pieces made at the Syracuse Stoneware Company in Syracuse, New York, circa 1890. Chamber pots and mixing bowls are the two most commonly seen forms with this banding. Since this colander is unique at this time, it may have been an experimental piece. $1,500.00 and up.

The pepper pots shown are all rare or unique examples. Although mocha decoration is considered difficult to find, the banded pots here would be more difficult to locate.

These pots were not always for pepper. Have you noticed how the holes can be large and/or in abundance? Sometimes the pots were used for sugar. This is where the name castor sugar comes from. A castor is another name for a pepper pot, hence, castor sugar. It was popular to mix cinnamon and sugar and use it on foods of all kinds, and these pots were the vessel used.

Far left: Possibly United States, due to the thickness and consistency of the clay. Blue-gray, black, and white bands. Note that the slip band is directly under the holes instead of sitting on top of the rim. Nineteenth century. $1,250.00 and up.

Left: Oxblood and white slip enameled, England, circa 1830. $950.00 and up.

Left: Dark green and white bands, England, circa 1830. $1,250.00 and up. Right: Heavy brown seaweed with blue and black bands, England, 1840 – 1870. $1,450.00 and up.

Pepper pots did not have a matching salt shaker, but rather a master salt. Master salts are usually bowl forms, with or without pedestal bases. It is possible to match master salts and pepper pots, but this is difficult, showing that they were *not* produced as sets but sold separately. Master salt is the accepted term for these pieces, but a more correct usage would be salt dip or open salt. The term "master salt" meant just that, a salt for the master. True master salts were big — bigger than the salts shown here. England and United States, 1830 – 1900.

Not the typical master salt form, this salt also has much thicker potting. $450.00 – 550.00.

A selection of blue, white, and blue and white banded master salts, with a banded and engine-turned example second from left. $475.00 – 650.00 each.

This rare American master salt was produced in a mold intended for glass, not pottery. $550.00 – 650.00.

English banded master salts exhibiting the three major forms. $475.00 – 650.00 each.

Left: American Rockingham-decorated master salt, Ohio or Indiana. Mid to late 1900s. $325.00 – 450.00 Right, English master salt, 1890 – 1920. $250.00 – 300.00.

T.G. Green produced pieces decorated in an identical fashion, circa 1900, although this salt does have an earlier look to it. $425.00 – 525.00.

These two salts are interesting because they have wide slip bands, as opposed to the typical combination of narrow slip bands. The salt on the right has an unusual concave-shaped bowl. Each, $475.00 – 650.00.

An early English flask, circa 1840. The shallow, finely molded detail is on both sides of this round vessel. $850.00 – 1,250.00.

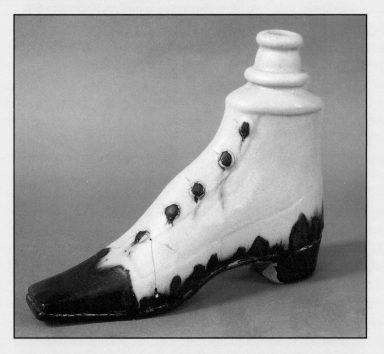

This bottle was probably for shoe or boot polish, as the figure is holding a cloth in one hand and a boot over the opposite arm. The ceramic top would have completed the rest of his hat and would have had a cork or wood stopper to be inserted into the opening of the bottle. England, third quarter nineteenth century. $450.00 – 550.00.

Shoe bottles are usually Rockingham-decorated, so this shoe is very different. The glaze highlighting the buttons and base is black with a greenish cast. England, late 1800s. $450.00 – 550.00.

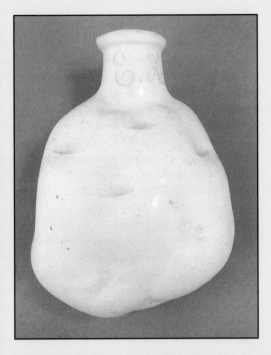

Potato flasks found to date measure from 4" to 8" long. The Rockingham-decorated example is the most common (Book 1); the personalized examples shown are unique at this time. Potatoes are used in making vodka. Both, England, circa 1870 – 1880. Small plain potato with incised initials on neck, $495.00 – 625.00. Cobalt-decorated potato with cobalt initials, $650.00 – 795.00.

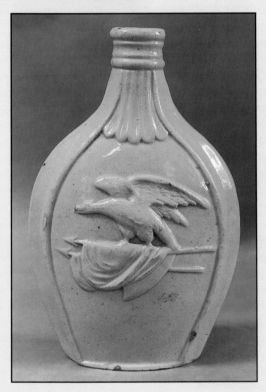

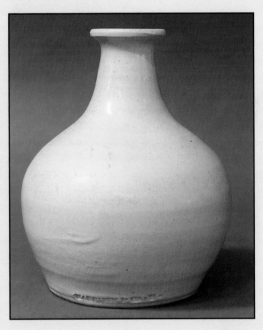

An American bottle or flask showing an eagle with flags on one side and morning glories on the other. The detail tends to be very good on these pieces when found. This bottle has also been found with Rockingham decoration. 7¼" high. $1,000.00 and up.

This 7" high bottle is marked "HARRISON & CAsH" at the base. This may have been a vendor's mark; there is a history of vendors' marks on pottery, and research reveals no potteries by that name. Of the two examples found to date, both were found in New Hampshire. (See Potters' Marks.) $525.00 – 650.00.

Two mocha-decorated tankards: The unusual small size has blue squiggly slip – generally, those bands are white; the normal tankard size has predominately orange earthworm and the unusual bands are pale blue and speckled with cobalt. Left: United States, circa 1855, $1,000.00 and up. Right: England, circa 1830, $1,850.00 and up.

Plain yellow ware shaving mug from East Liverpool, Ohio. The primitive appearance is due to poor molding and overfiring in the kiln. 1850 – 1890. $350.00 – 450.00.

Oversized handled cup and saucer, about 6½" in diameter. Possibly for serving soup or mush, nineteenth century Austria or Germany. $350.00 – 450.00.

Transfers on yellow ware are very difficult to find. This is a child's mug, 2¼" high, with a charming scene of a boy and his dog, circa 1840. England. $450.00 – 550.00.

This brown and white slip-banded goblet is unique at this time. Bennington produced Rockingham-decorated goblets that are small and straight-sided; this goblet is probably English because of its style. An exceptional piece. 7" high, 1850 – 1890. $1,000.00 and up.

Plain yellow porringer, England, circa 1850. Remember that, since a porringer is for eating, it will not have a flat rim, like a potty. Porringers can be found in various sizes and date at least to the late eighteenth century. $450.00 – 550.00.

Handleless teacups or tea bowls, England, circa 1840, with cornflower blue and black flowers. These cups would have had matching saucers. Each, $100.00 – 135.00.

This slim tankard may have been a practice piece because it exhibits many different techniques. The slip bands are blue, brown, and black, wide and narrow; it has a fanciful handle and an applied decoration of leaves with green oxide. England, circa 1840 – 1850. $650.00 – 850.00.

Possibly for a church, this chalice is almost 7" high, and the bowl is 6½" in diameter. A rare form. The stem is too tall for this piece to be a compote. United States, nineteenth century. $650.00 and up.

This presentation mug or cup is not only rare, but an important study piece. It is the earliest known dated yellow ware: "Sept. 20, 1822," one year after Thomas Sharpe opened his pottery in Derbyshire, England, where he produced earthenware and stoneware. It is not known what relationship Edmund Sharpe bore to Thomas Sharpe, if any. The date allows us to learn that banded yellow ware is earlier than previously thought. The frog is flatter than usual, with an open smiling mouth. $2,000.00 and up.

Child's mug with pink lustre bird in a tree. England, circa 1840. $450.00 – 550.00.

Rare black scenic transfer mug, England, circa 1830 – 1840. The transfer on this mug is excellent, crisp and intense, extending into the mug and onto the handle. The mark is also done by means of transfer (See Potters' Marks). $550.00 – 750.00.

This blue seaweed-decorated cup and saucer is so small that it may have been used for demitasse. The word "demitasse," defined as serving strong black coffee after dinner, was coined 1835 – 1845, the same age as this cup and saucer. These two pieces would be worth buying separately. England or Scotland. $1,500.00 and up for the set.

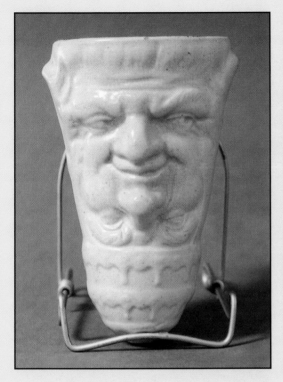 

Stirrup cups were used during the hunt, to put in the rider's pocket and be available at a moment's notice. Right side up, you see the pope; upside down (and in drinking position!), you see the devil. White-lined. The first Pope and Devil stirrup cups were produced about 1790; this one dates circa 1825. 5" high. $950.00 and up.

French porringer, circa 1840 – 1850. This cup seems too stylish to be an everyday porridge cup. Porringers weren't just for porridge (oatmeal) but also for soups and stews. They were replaced by drinking cups and bowls not long after this cup was made. $450.00 – 550.00.

Frogs in mugs and pitchers were supposed to frighten the drinker and make him stop drinking. Whether they did or not is anybody's guess. Lizards were also used for this purpose, alone or in conjunction with frogs. Mugs with frogs were made primarily in the United States and England. When you see a mug, you never know if there might be a frog inside.

From the outside, this is an ordinary mug from Ohio, circa 1880. The band pattern is the most common one you will find. Inside, though, is a huge frog in the act of jumping out of the mug. The frog looks suspended in midair; in fact, there is very little room for liquid at all. $950.00 and up.

This mug exhibits a grapevine design that can be found on mugs of many sizes, from child-size to ones like this large 5" example. Most of them don't have a nice frog with a realistically done Rockingham glaze. The origin of this mug keeps the price below that of an American-made example. England, 1850 – 1880. $750.00 – 950.00.

A small tankard, banded in russet, blue, and brown, with the addition of rouletted bands in the center. Generally, rouletted bands are at the rim of a mug or tankard, and highlighted with a glaze. England, circa 1830. $1,100.00 – 1,450.00.

A rather primitive mug, with two wavy white bands on a russet band, surrounded by wide blue and brown slip bands. The speckled blue band and the wavy lines date the mug to circa 1830, England. Oversized at 5 by 5½". $1,750.00 and up.

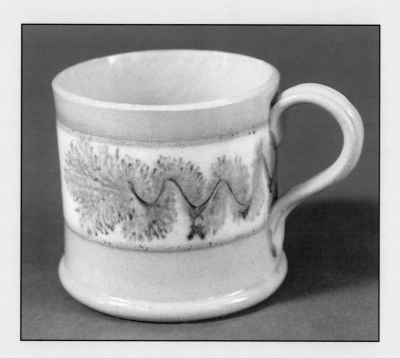

The most common mocha-decorated mug will have blue, brown and/or white slip bands, and blue seaweed in no distinct pattern. United States, England, or Canada, circa 1870. $495.00 – 695.00.

Flower Pots and Related Forms

Most of the yellow ware baskets found are stoneware with a yellow glaze. Few are real yellow ware, like this basket. A very difficult piece to locate, so condition is not as important as it would be on a later basket. Nineteenth century. $750.00 and up.

At some point in production, the Weller pottery discontinued making these flower frogs in yellow ware and started making them in stoneware with a bright yellow glaze, so look closely when purchasing. This was the simplest form produced; look for frog-shaped flower frogs as well. Circa 1930. $25.00 – 35.00.

This planter was made in two different sizes, in Ohio, circa 1930 – 1940. Recently, the design was revived and reproduced in an unglazed yellow version. The few antique barrels I have seen are golden yellow clay and glazed. The planter shown is the largest size at 12" high. The 12" measurment is an estimate, based on memory of this 1990 polaroid. $650.00 and up.

The root of the word "jardinière" is jardin…garden. The earliest yellow ware jardinières were produced in Ohio, by many of the potteries, around 1915. Production of these continued for about 20 years. Since jardinières were meant to be ornamental, the clay is embossed and covered with colored glaze. The most desirable examples will show yellow clay through the glaze, and will be difficult to find. The embossed and green-highlighted example is unique at this time. Each, $475.00 – 795.00, depending on size.

Flower Pots and Related Forms

Yellow ware flowerpots are not common, even though they were produced for almost 100 years. The earlier examples, containing no stoneware, were easily broken and damaged. They were small, too, about 5" high. The pink lustre example with the house, and the sanded (yes, real sand) pot with saucer, date about 1830 – 1940 and are English. The green oxide and Rockingham examples are patent dated "SEP 1924." The patent for this flowerpot was issued to John H. Pettit and John J. Fitzpatrick of Vienna, West Virginia. The application stated that they had, amongst other ideas, invented a way to solve drainage problems by creating three pockets that would perform the duties of a saucer. Their flowerpots were produced in at least two different sizes.

$550.00 – 650.00

$650.00 – 800.00

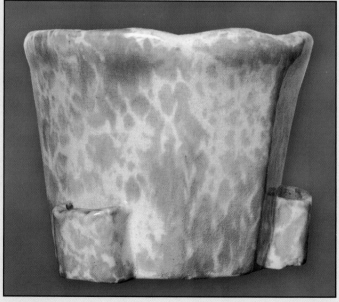

$250.00 – 400.00, depending on size.

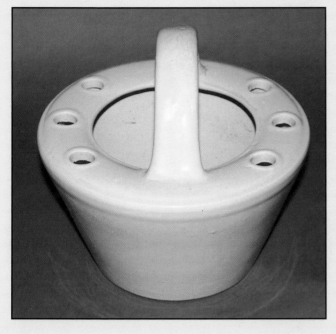

This 1930s yellow ware/stoneware basket is appealing in its simplicity. The verge with six holes is an unusual feature. The handle is so low that it would be difficult to put flowers in the center. This may be the reason for the holes: easier access. Possibly made for the display of pansies. Ohio. $350.00 – 450.00.

Quintal vases, so-called because of their five fingers, were originally made to display tulips. Most commonly found in pearlware, there have been only two yellow ware examples found. They are an early English form, c. 1825. This quintal has a nearly solid Rockingham glaze, which was popular at the time to use in decorating yellow ware. $500.00 and up.

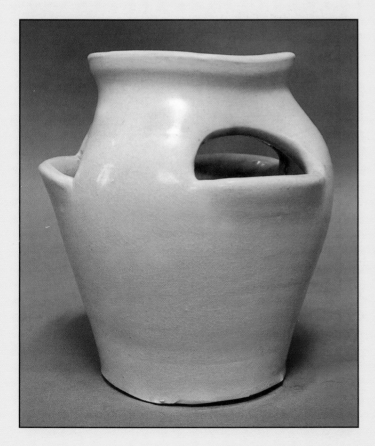

Strawberry jars, like this one, were produced in yellow ware as well as stoneware with a yellow glaze. The yellow glaze on the stoneware pieces is bright chrome yellow. Various Ohio potteries made pieces like this jar in the 1930s. $150.00 – 200.00.

The figural pieces shown here are mostly decorative. Dogs are the most commonly repre-sented animal, with pigs, frogs and lions tying for second. The earliest yellow ware figural pieces were produced circa 1800 in England and Scotland; by 1900 figural yellow ware pieces were no longer produced. The only exception is animal banks, mostly pigs and frogs, which were made in the midwest through the first quarter of the twentieth century. Human figures are rarely found (except as the Austrian smoking stands). Most of the English figural pieces were produced using a pearlware (white earthenware) body; the yellow ware bodies may have been experimental or curiosities. This is a challenging collecting area because it is difficult to find figural yellow ware, but worth it, if you enjoy animals.

East Liverpool, Ohio, lion doorstop. These lions were also produced as inkwells, with the holes in the base alongside the lion. If a doorstop, the base will be hollow. They can be found with Rockingham or blue oxide glaze as well as plain yellow ware. $1,450.00 and up.

Early English figures, probably toys at the sizes of 3" and 4" high, respectively. Both are hollow. Circa 1825. $495.00 – 650.00 each.

The Rockingham-glazed dog doorstop is the most common animal found, however, this is a rare exam-ple. The rarest feature is the forward facing posi-tion. The dog has a smooth face and a long nose and less of a curly spaniel look. The base was origi-nally produced as a baking/serving dish. An excep-tional yellow ware dog. East Liverpool, Ohio, circa 1860. $3,000.00 and up.

Since many yellow ware dogs were produced in Ohio, these are rare because they were made in New York. The glaze is solid, so they were obviously dipped in Rockingham, instead of dripped or sponged. Marked "JORDAN." (See Potters' Marks.) $3,800.00 and up for the pair.

An unusual dog because it was made without a base. The small, separate foreleg is different, too. Face and body detail is of very good quality. Probably Yorkshire, England, circa 1860. May have been made as a pair. $750.00 – 850.00.

Morrison and Crawford (Rosslyn Pottery) in Kirkcaldy, Scotland, was well-known for glazing yellow ware in this combination of brown, green, and blue glazes. This pig was a favorite form of other potteries in the town as well; it is famous as a Wemyss (weems) pig. This pig is a bank, circa 1860. $450.00 – 550.00.

These two pig-shaped banks show the difference in form between Scottish pottery from Kirkcaldy, and eastern Ohio potteries, even though the glazes are similar. Left, $295.00 – 395.00. Right, $175.00 – 275.00.

English hollow reclining stag, circa 1825, with Rockingham daubing. Modelled after Staffordshire figures from 1780 to 1800. 5" long. $850.00 – 1,100.00.

These small, colorful figures are match holders. Just under 5" high, the striking area for the match is either roughly molded or unglazed, both shown here. Swedish and English, respectively, mid to late 1800s. Each, $450.00 – 550.00.

Pair of hollow lions, male and female, with a splash of Rockingham. Note the circular designs pressed into the bodies and bases. This would have been done with a tool made of wood or metal. The clay is thin and a deep yellow. About 4" long each and made in England, circa 1825. $1,250.00 – 1,500.00 for the pair.

Distinctive Yorkshire colors on this figure of a reclining lamb. England, circa 1810, 4" long. $750.00 – 950.00.

Paperweights in the form of frogs on bases. Both are American and date 1850 – 1880. Sized to fit the hand. Each, $350.00 – 450.00.

Small, Victorian figure of a child hugging her dog. This may have been a toy for a child. The gilding is identical to that found on Continental smoking stands and pin boxes. $225.00 – 295.00.

Unique at this time, this life-size deer head with holes for the antlers of your choice. Realistic molding, even the teeth. The head hung by a wire, inserted at the pottery, which can be partially seen below the neck. Nineteenth century. $1,200.00 and up.

This larger-than-usual yellow ware bank has yellow in the glaze, giving it a tan colored appearance. It had black overglaze painted details, mostly worn off now, which could have been done at the factory. About 6½" high, the origin is Continental, circa 1880. $550.00 – 675.00.

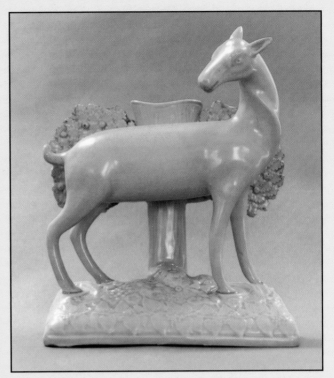

Enoch Wood, an active potter in 1820s England, could have made this large stag with spill holder. Branching out from the spill holder on each side is a bocage, or tree, a typical ornament of this period. A great figure, unique at this time. $2,200.00 and up.

This figure represents Thomas Dartmouth Rice playing "Jim Crow." Rice blackened his face with burnt cork, and sang and danced portraying an elderly African-American. His act was instantly popular in the United States, and he performed at the Royal Surrey Theatre in London in 1833. This rare figure is obviously in commemoration of his visit to England. 6" high, with Rockingham decoration, the most common decoration on yellow ware figures of this period. $1,350.00 – 1,650.00.

The subject matter of some figures is taken from everyday life. This figure group depicts bull baiting, a popular sport in England at the time this figure was made, circa 1825. Unique in yellow ware at this time. 8½" long. $4,000.00 and up.

While this is a standard form for an Ohio dog doorstop, everything else about it is unusual. The decoration is well done, with touches of Rockingham and white slip, especially on the dog's face. The molded base has been left undecorated. The information on the base is a treasure: "Made at J H Knowles East Liverpool March 26 1867." Also incised in script is "Try SPJ." "SPJ." is most likely the initials of the potter. 10¾"high. $4,000.00 and up.

"Street Musicians" is the name of this Yorkshire, England, figure group. It consists of a man playing the triangle, a ram, an odd looking lion-dog, and a monkey wearing a hat and playing a horn. Circus groups were a big attraction with the public, because they provided entertainment, and the groups earned money by performing. The yellow clay body is decorated with green and brown glazes, colors that were used 1790 – 1810. The group is rare in decorated pearlware, rarer still in yellow clay. $5,000.00 and up.

A unique figure of Jumbo the Elephant, 10" high and 10" long. Jumbo spent the first 20 years of his life at the London Zoo. P.T. Barnum paid $10,000 for him, and Jumbo arrived in New York City in 1882 to join the circus. He was 12 feet tall and weighed approximately seven tons. He was the top attraction at Barnum's circus until his death in 1885. This figure has a rare mark of "The Globe Pottery Co." (See Potters' Mark for more information on the Globe Pottery Co.) $4,000.00 and up.

This majestic male dog, 16" long and 16" high, is the largest yellow ware animal ever found. It was exhibited at Williamsburg during the 1960s. The dog has great details: a trim, smooth body, a standing position, and an upright tail with a "coleslaw" tip to imitate fur. The face has a primitive expression. The Rockingham was skillfully applied, and the cushion base is decorated with the glaze that dripped from the dog's body. It's difficult to imagine, but this dog is life-size. This is an incredible piece of pottery, yellow ware or not, so the value transcends being yellow ware as we know it. England, circa 1850. $15,000.00 and up.

Scottish multiglaze dog doorstop, circa 1860. Rather primitive, with a combination of molded and hand-modelled details. Unusual square base. 7" high. $950.00 – 1,250.00.

Another example of a great East Liverpool, Ohio, dog doorstop. It has a bi-colored glaze of Rockingham and teal blue, and a huge base embossed with the figures of dogs. 12¼" high, with a base measuring 7½" x 10½". Circa 1865. $3,000.00 and up.

Edward Tunnicliff potted in the United States in East Liverpool, Ohio; Zanesville, Ohio; and Kewa-nee, Ohio. He came from England in 1839 at the beginning of yellow ware production. In Zanesville he made Rockingham, most of which is marked. Tunnicliff made utilitarian pieces, such as jars, mugs and teapots, and figural pieces like this pair of greyhounds or whippets. He also made other dogs and a bust of George Washington. This pair of dogs is very sophisticated for yellow ware and is in the style of Staffordshire dogs of similar vintage. The Rockingham glaze is highly evolved and has a metallic cast. It is nearly impossible to put a price on yellow ware pieces such as these dogs. However, were they available for sale, their value would easily exceed $20,000. Length, 10½", height 6½".

Crisp black seaweed on this English covered sugar bowl. Circa 1870. $1,350.00 – 1,650.00.

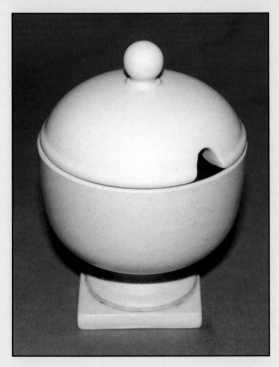

Gresley Ware mustard pot, England, 1950s. The smaller-than-usual size makes it easy to pick up without a handle. $225.00 – 295.00.

An unusual form, this mustard pot is stamped "WEDGWOOD." Although it has a classical look, it was produced about 1930. $350.00 – 450.00.

Rare Rebekah at the Well sugar bowl. This is a piece worth buying without a cover. Probably E. and W. Bennett, Baltimore, Maryland, since marked examples exist from this pottery. I am also attributing this to Bennett because of the quality of the glaze and the potting. (See the Rebekah at the Well teapot for more information.) The base is not corrugated, so this piece was produced circa 1850 – 1870. $450.00 – 550.00.

Since most mustard pots are decorated, this one is unusual in its plainness. The finials are normally flat, mushroom shapes. England, 1840 – 1880. $495.00 – 625.00.

It's difficult to remember, in these days of plastic containers and aluminum pans, that food storage and cooking vessels were once mainly ceramic and wood. The wooden pieces burned, rotted, and fell apart. However, 100 to 150 years later, I can (and do) still use yellow ware baking dishes and covered crocks.

Some pieces in this chapter had lids that were broken while removing them, such as wax sealers. Some had tin lids, or cork or carved wooden stoppers, all of which were easily thrown away or damaged. The pottery lids that, by some good fortune, are still with their bases may be in rough condition.

At the store, medicine, liquor, or candy may have been packaged in a ceramic container. And since one didn't know that it was going to be an antique one day, the ceramic container was thrown away when it was empty (outhouses were used as dumps and can contain wonderful ceramic treasures).

This chapter contains a wide array of storage and cooking pieces. Being in the kitchen would be great if you had all of these yellow ware pieces to use!

Small straight-sided jars for medicines. The tin lids are missing. United States, nineteenth century. $50.00 – 110.00 each.

Scalloped-edge baking dish with a faintly embossed design. Not a common form. 11" long, United States, 1850 – 1880. $395.00 – 495.00.

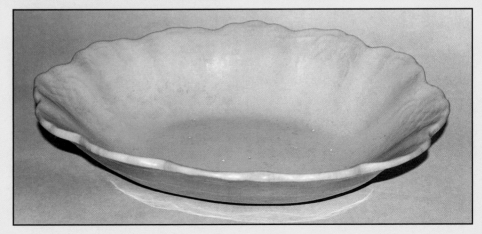

Large crock with heavy embossing and draped, classical heads for handles. This crock would have had a lid. Highly refined clay with a high glaze. Possibly Ohio, 1850 – 1880. $350.00 – 450.00, without lid.

This large, barrel-shaped jar resembles a canning jar, but its missing lid would not have been the type to seal the contents. 7" high, 5½" in diameter. United States. $225.00 – 295.00, with lid.

This plain yellow keeler is embossed to resemble wood. It can be found in three different sizes and came with a bail handle with a black-painted wooden grip. United States, 1850 – 1890. $350.00 – 450.00, regardless of size.

Rare Rockingham-decorated syrup pitcher, probably Ohio, 1850 – 1870. Depending on price, this is a form well worth purchasing without the metal top. It might be possible to fit another metal top on the syrup pitcher. $495.00 – 595.00.

This bottle or large cruet is strikingly 1930s, by its form. 8" high. United States $225.00 – 295.00.

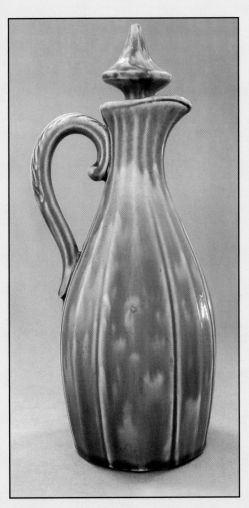

Ohio cruet with pottery stopper, third quarter nineteenth century. Don't expect the stopper to fit exactly. As with most pieces with pottery lids or stoppers, the tops were made on different days and sometimes by a different potter than made the base. $495.00 – 595.00.

Although this white-banded cookie jar is a later form, it is not easy to find. Watt Pottery, Ohio, circa 1930. $250.00 – 350.00.

Some English pieces, like this covered jar, have Rockingham at the rim only. 7½" high. Circa 1900. $125.00 – 175.00.

The width of the bands and the sparse blue seaweed identify this jar as made in Ohio. The tall, cylindrical form is not an easy one to find, and the domed lid adds to the overall design. About 7½" tall, circa 1880. $1,250.00 and up.

The "handles' on this small crock identify it as English: applied shells with a rope design. They are covered with white slip. This could have been a sugar bowl; if so, it may have been an open sugar and would not have had a lid. 1840 – 1870. $350.00 – 450.00 as shown.

These round tureens are two of only three known yellow ware forms decorated with mocha (see Book 2, pg. 99, for the third example). This form can also be found in pearlware with mocha decoration, but it is more rare in yellow ware. These may have been special order pieces because there are so few, and they would not have been a form that got hard wear or broke easily. It is interesting that, even though they are all decorated with blue seaweed and slip bands, each one is unique. The handles on the dot-seaweed example are identical to the lift lug on the Lock-Up pitcher (Book 2, pg. 125), which is dated 1846. $6,500.00 and up each.

This English ovoid jar is rare because of its pierced base. Although the exact usage is not known, it may have been for leeches. The foliated, open strap handles are an odd looking addition, but they did enable the user to get a firmer grip than solid, ear-shaped handles. 6" high, 1840 – 1860. $1,450.00 and up.

The covered crock form is common, but the plum and blue slip bands are not. 6" in diameter. United States, 1890 – 1920. $350.00 – 450.00.

The blue slip bands on this pear-shaped jar highlight the raised bands on the body of the jar. The raised bands were sometimes referred to as "hooped" and could be either molded or hand-cut. Nicely embossed ear-shaped handles. This piece would have had a lid. United States or England, 1860 – 1890. $ 450.00 – 550.00, with lid.

This canister is part of the Cornish Gold line. Invented circa 1967 by Judith Onions, a designer for T. G. Green, the line included kitchenware and dinnerware. Plates and cups for the table, bowls and pitchers for use in the kitchen, were just some of the forms produced. A variety of shakers were made, including labeled ones for salt, pepper, flour, and sugar. The clay is a mix of yellow ware and stoneware and the bands are always white slip. Cornish Gold was made for at least ten years, but not thought to be in production today. Later pieces like these have merit, but care should be paid to the purchase price. Two-pint household jar, $95.00 – 135.00.

Low, covered jar, molded to look like a sunflower, with a tripod finial. About 6" in diameter. 1850 – 1890. $550.00 – 650.00.

This form is familiar, a yellow ware storage jar, but the glaze is a rare combination of ochre, and a blue and white daubed design. 5" tall and probably eastern Ohio, circa 1880. $550.00 – 650.00.

The basis for this jar was a teapot form. The pineapple and daisy design is crisp and unique. There is no way of knowing what the lid would have looked like, or the jar's intended purpose. United States circa 1870. $550.00 – 650.00.

This Rockingham-decorated batter jug is identical in form to a stoneware batter jug. Making it in yellow ware may have been experimental. It would have had a tin lid and tin spout cover. New York or Pennsylvania, circa 1870. $550.00 – 650.00.

An earlier example than most egg separators found. The clay is not so refined nor highly glazed as the 1980s versions. It could be pre-1900 since it is not marked. England. $95.00 – 125.00.

An early cat's eye mocha-decorated jar. The thin, pale clay and the rouletted bands, along with the cat's eye decoration, date it to circa 1810. England, 6" high. $1,500.00 and up.

Jars of this form are often called humidors, but their exact purpose is unknown. These two examples have excellent glaze, and great contrast. They are American and date from 1850 to 1880. On the left is probably the largest example you could find, a whopping 13½" high and 11" in diameter, with Rockingham and turquoise-blue glaze. $1,100.00 – 1,400.00. On the right, 8" high by 5" in diameter, with Rockingham and green glaze. $450.00 – 550.00.

Almost 9" high, this rare, tall crock has a strong presence because of the deep yellow clay and multiple deep brown bands. The slip covered finial is unusual, and the handles are similar to that of lift lugs on large pitchers. Worth buying without a lid. Probably Ohio, 1840 – 1870. $1,500.00 and up.

These are some examples of the wheat-embossed spice canisters produced by the Hull Pottery in Crooksville, Ohio, circa 1925. They are about 3¾" tall. Carrollton Pottery in Carrollton, Ohio used an "H" in a diamond mark as well as Hull, but their "H" is vertical inside the diamond. Also, Carrollton Pottery was not known for making yellow ware. For more information about wheat-embossed canisters, see pg. 98 in Book 2. $295.00 – 395.00. each.

Staffordshire potters, beginning in the 1860s, originally produced hand-painted hen tureens in white pottery. Their purpose was to keep boiled eggs warm. The two yellow ware examples shown were meant to be more decorative than practical. The Rockingham and green glazed hen is European; the Rockingham-only hen may be American. Each between 7" and 8" long. 1860 – 1880. $650.00 – 850.00 each.

Covered tureens that resemble this quail, with a bright yellow ware body and brown-glazed base, were most likely candy dishes. Hens and ducks are also found, in sizes from 3" to 9" long. The larger examples are marked on the base with a group of letters and numbers. 1930+, and most likely England or Europe. Quail, 9" long. $225.00 – 295.00.

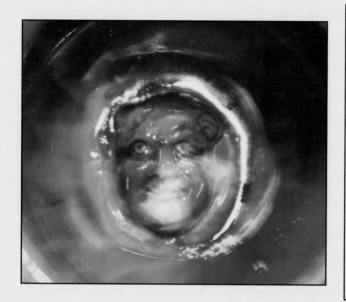

Bennington Pottery (Vermont) pipkin, with the rare addition of a face inside the base, made between 1847 and 1858. $700.00 – 850.00.

Lustre decoration on yellow ware is rarely found. The dates for production appear to be three separate periods: circa 1830 – 1840 (England), circa 1870s (eastern United States), and circa 1920 – 1930 (Ohio and California). The nappy shown is from the middle period. It has a wonderful stag design inside and out. $575.00 and up.

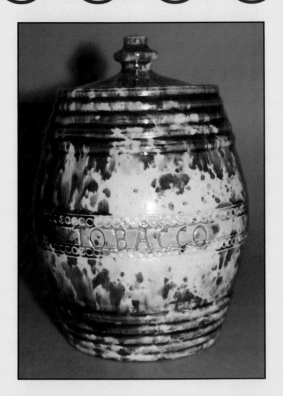

Morrison and Crawford's Rosslyn Pottery, Kirkcaldy Scotland, produced many yellow ware pieces with this tri-colored glaze, which they called majolica. The glaze was applied using broom twigs, and each color was applied separately. The two main areas of production were kitchenware and banks. The banks are animal, cottage, and geometric forms. The kitchenware pieces are bread containers and graduated canisters (see pg. 99, Book 2, for canisters). The canisters are barrel-shaped, ribbed top and bottom, with the name of the intended contents in applied letters in the middle. At times the letters were covered with white slip. Sugar, flour, rice, meal, and sago are some of the names found. Occasionally found are smaller canisters, about 5" to 6" high, with the name "TOBACCO." All pieces are circa 1860. These multiglazed pieces are often confused with the works of some United States potteries.

This small canister for tobacco has rouletted decoration and an incised name, as opposed to the usual applied name. $550.00 – 650.00.

This ware is called dabbed ware or dabbity ware. Brown, blue, and green were sponged on the entire exterior surface except for a small area in the front center. That area was reserved for a name, or Scottish saying, and a date. The name and date were inlaid directly onto the body using red clay. The forms are covered canisters. Seaton Pottery, Aberdeen, Scotland. $175.00 – 350.00, depending on size.

The bread safes are large, rectangular boxes, decorated with embossed trailing vines and leaves. The top of the lid has raised letters that spell out "BREAD" on two sides. The glaze usually obscures the beautiful details. $1,100.00 – 1,450.00.

This unique piece, which started life as a lowly milk pan, is attributed to William Bromley. Bromley was a Cincinnati, Ohio, potter from 1849 to about 1860. He was known for the type of elaborate designs represented by this milk pan. The dark blue seaweed, while not too crisp, is plentiful. The brown slip bands are so dark that they look black. The applied eagle is 3" to 4" in diameter and obviously dried out prior to firing. If you look closely, you will see that it is a great depiction of an eagle. $6,500.00 and up.

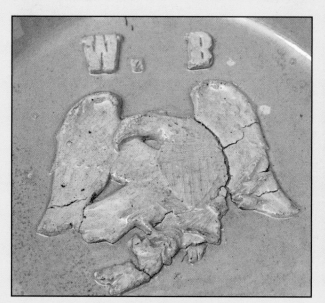

A cover for "CAKE," banded in the style of Brush-McCoy Dandy Line, was either a special order or experimental. The embossed band is unique on Dandy Line pieces. An exciting find! $2,000.00 and up.

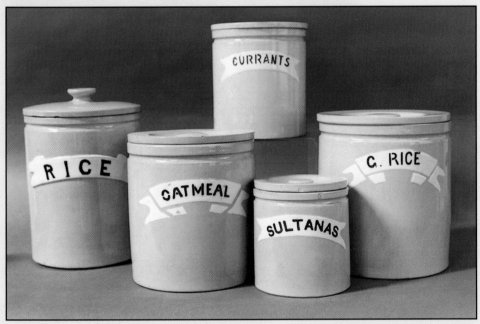

Yellow ware canisters in this style were produced in quantity by at least two English potteries. They are Lovatt & Lovatt, Langley Mill, and J. Bourne & Son, Denby. The Lovatt pieces date 1895 to 1931, the Bourne pieces, 1850 to about 1930. (Interestingly, J. Bourne & Son, Ltd., acquired Lovatt & Lovatt in 1959.) The Lovatt pieces have these characteristics: a higher percentage of yellow clay, recessed lid finials, flat white band. (Lovatt pieces may also be impressed "LEADLESS GLAZE") The Bourne pieces have more of a stoneware body, a raised white band, and a finial set above the lid. The sizes found to date are 4" to 9" high. Prices on these pieces have risen, fueled by demand for white banded pieces with names, and the lack of Dandy Line pieces available to fill that demand. $150.00 – 450.00 , depending on size and name.

Below is a partial list of names to be found on canisters:

RICE	SAGO	TEA	SEMOLINA
G. (Ground) RICE	CANDIED PEEL	SUGAR	BEANS
OATMEAL	FLOUR	BARLEY	
CURRANTS	MEAL	PEAS	
SULTANAS	MIXED PEEL	RAISINS	

This pear-shaped jar was for snuff, a powdered form of tobacco. The base has an unusual mark, with advertising within a raised medallion of the jar itself. (See Potters' Marks.) Since the jar is marked Baltimore (Maryland) and there were yellow ware potteries there, it is possible to attribute this jar to one of the potteries there. There was a Phoenix Pottery in East Liverpool, Ohio who produced plain yellow snuff jars. This pottery, run by William Brunt, Jr., & Co., may have also been the maker. A ridge inside the rim, shows that there was a lid of some type. On the two jars found, neither has had the lid. This could mean that the lid was not pottery, not considered valuable or perhaps made of wood or wax and therefore considered dispensable. Circa 1850, 7" high. $350.00 – 450.00.

The form on this canning jar is not rare, but few yellow ware collectors have ever seen a jar with a locking lid. The finial was easy to grip, being hexagonal. The raised areas on the lid edge fitted under the tabs, on the inner rim of the jar, when the lid was turned. United States, 1850 – 1880. $295.00 – 395.00.

Rockingham over blue seaweed was an experimental Ohio production. Bowls can also be found with this decoration. East Liverpool, Ohio potteries, circa 1880. $495.00 – 650.00.

A unique design on yellow ware. The predominately blue earthworm was made to resemble branching coral. The banded sections are also exceptional. The fine blue and white lines have gaps showing the yellow clay, so they resemble tri-colored bands. This pitcher is the work of a highly skilled potter. England, circa 1825. $4,000.00 and up.

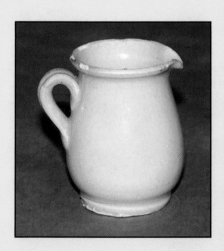

Miniature or toy pitcher, Scandinavian or European origin. Yellow ware from this part of the world may be a different shade of yellow. Recognizing this may help you to determine origin and maker on other yellow ware pieces. About 2½" high. nineteenth century. $175.00 – 250.00.

It looks as if there is something missing on this pitcher. We are used to seeing multiple, multicolored slip bands and/or seaweed. Whether by design or accident, this simple pitcher has just one wide band. 6½" high. Ohio, 1870 – 1900. $600.00 – 795.00.

An English pitcher with black transfer scenes of daily life. The transfers look like an afterthought, extending over the blue slip bands, instead of being between them. Rouletted decoration along with the transfers dates this pitcher to circa 1830. $595.00 – 795.00.

The "agate" mocha design on this English pitcher is rarely seen. It was achieved by rolling dried bits of variegated clay or slip onto the surface of the pitcher. This technique was used in the 1790s on pearlware, so I would date this pitcher no later than 1810. The pitchers that are found are this shape only, and range from 3" to 6" in height. They have medium blue bands and are white-lined. 6" pitcher, $1,500.00 and up. If this seems like a low price for such a rare mocha decoration, it is because it has not yet caught the eye of popular demand.

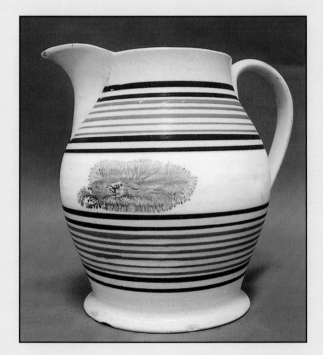

This pitcher is very striking, because the blue and brown slip bands cover much of the pitcher's surface. The impact of the bands offsets the negligible blue seaweed. 7½" high. Ohio or England. $1,450.00 – 1,650.00.

Ohio potteries produced embossed pitchers like these in the first quarter of the twentieth century. They differ in style from the many embossed pitchers produced in the third quarter of the nineteenth century. These two pitchers have designs that are not commonly found on yellow ware. They were dipped in bi-colored slip, another unusual decorative technique. The pitcher on the left, a Dutch boy and girl with windmill, was produced in blue and white stoneware as well as yellow ware. Each, $225.00 – 295.00.

The form of this pitcher determined the placement of the bands. Probably Ohio, circa 1870. 7½" high. $850.00 – 950.00.

The decoration on this barrel-shaped pitcher is called dipped and engine-turned. The pitcher would have been dipped in one or more colors of slip and then cut, or engine-turned, on a machine with multiple blades. The blades cut away the slip, revealing the yellow clay, and thus creating the pattern on the body of the pitcher. This method of decorating pottery was invented in England in the late eighteenth century. The addition of the reeded bands, covered with green oxide, and the russet slip bands, make this a visually exciting piece. $5,000.00 and up.

An ewer is defined as a pitcher with a wide spout. This is the typical form found with a basin – a bowl and pitcher set. The use of black places origin around the Yorkshire area, England, circa 1810. The circles were stamped or sponged on very closely together. $950.00 – 1,250.00.

Although unmarked, this 5" pitcher was probably made by the Pacific Clay Products Co., in Los Angeles, California. This pitcher dates approximately, 1921 – 1935, but the company was making yellow ware as early as the late 1800s. This mark can be found either impressed on stamped in ink. $350.00 – 450.00.

Toby jugs or pitchers were produced in England first, and then produced in the United States, in places like South Amboy, New Jersey, and Bennington, Vermont. This example is larger than usual, 10" high, with an exceptionally wide-brimmed hat. $795.00 – 895.00.

Earthworm, or cable, as potters called it, was produced by a slip cup with multiple chambers. The different chambers were for different colored slip, and a drop from this slip cup created a round design called cat's eye. The potter then overlapped the cat's eyes, creating a chain that could be looped or wavy. The pitcher on the left shows earthworm that is not well articulated and was obviously a practice piece. The earthworm on the right, while not perfect, is much better. The double chain of cable, along with the placement and color of the slip bands, elevate its price greatly. England, circa 1820. Left, $1,100.00 – 1,500.00: Right, $3,500.00 and up.

In the third quarter of the nineteenth century, Rockingham decoration was at its high point. In the first quarter of the twentieth century, embossed blue and white stoneware was produced by many midwestern potteries. Occasionally these potteries used the same molds for yellow ware. Both of these facts make it difficult to find plain yellow embossed pieces. There are hundreds of embossed designs found on yellow ware pitchers. Shown are a few unusual embossed patterns found with a yellow ware body.

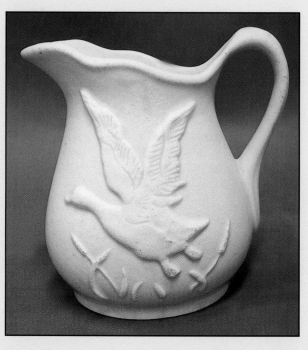

Castle (monastery) and Fish Scale, also produced in blue and white stoneware. This shows a building with a peaked roof and a cross, set against a scaled background. Various sizes produced in blue and white; this example is 7" high. White lined. $395.00 – 495.00.

This nineteenth century form shows a duck in flight. 9½". $450.00 – 550.00.

This pitcher, with an embossed pattern similar to a walnut shell, can be found in many sizes, from 4¾" to 9" high. The bamboo-style handle was an option. Sometimes the handle was completely smooth. A variety of colored glazes were used, including Rockingham and green oxides, singly or combined. Morton Pottery, Morton, Illinois, 1877 – 1917. $250.00 – 500.00, depending on size and coloration.

Beautiful Scottish pitcher, with a superb embossed pineapple design. This pitcher is representative of the fine work done by Scottish potters. Alloa Pottery. (See Potters' Marks for the mark and information about this pottery.) $850.00 and up.

This pitcher has an unusual shape as well, as an unusual design of daisies over what appears to be water lilies. It has been found in two sizes, 5" and 8" high. nineteenth century. $350.00 – 500.00, depending on size.

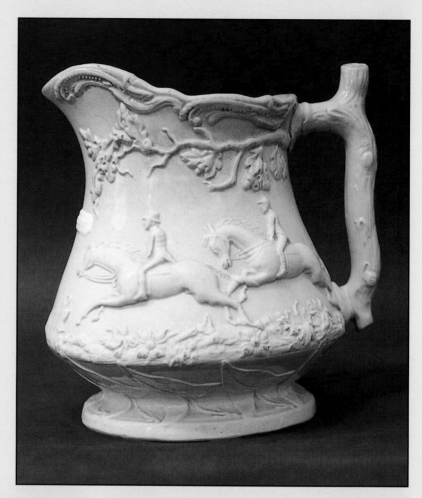

Most of the Swan Hill pitchers were decorated with Rockingham and/or Rockingham and blue glazes. This plain yellow example shows the artistry of Charles Coxon, with its crisp design. It was a presentation pitcher for "J Kennedy," who lived in south central Pennsylvania. The plaque with his name is different than on most presentation pitchers; the names were usually done in larger letters applied directly onto the surface of the pitcher. The "twig" handle is a Swan Hill characteristic. For more on Charles Coxon, and his mark, see Potters' Marks section. $4,500.00 and up.

Closeup of Swan Hill pitcher name plaque.

(Right) This form is called Hall Boy. It was produced by Brush-McCoy, circa 1920. It can be found in blue and white stoneware, blue and white spongeware, plain yellow, and yellow ware with Rockingham. This example with green glaze is unique at this time. $300.00 – 395.00.

 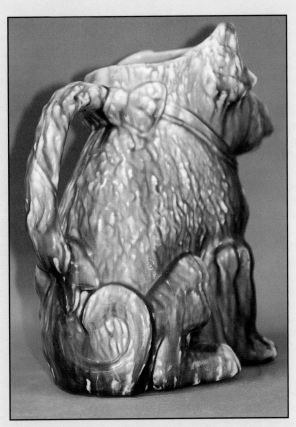

This dog-shaped pitcher has wonderful glaze and molded details. Nineteenth century, United States, 10" tall. $950.00 – 1,250.00.

A ewer with many brown and white bands, possibly United States. You can see where a piece was knocked loose before the slip was fully dry. Two slip cups were employed here: a triple tube cup for the white slip, and a double tube cup for the brown slip. Nineteenth century. $1,150.00 – 1,450.00.

Small Toby pitcher, with an unusually smooth, rounded body and a hound handle. The glaze is a brown wash or dip instead of the familiar sponged or dripped pattern. The slip "S" on the unglazed bottom may refer to Swan Hill Pottery, South Amboy, New Jersey About 5" high. $595.00 – 750.00.

A rarely seen mocha decoration, this dot-seaweed pattern was punched into the clay first, to guide the potter. The punch can be felt on the surface of the pitcher, and gives the illusion of a white dot in the center of some of the seaweed dots. There are four dot-seaweed patterns, in two colors, known at this time. The design, a crown, is an obvious English motif. It is unique at this time. There are six crowns on this pitcher. Circa 1830. $3,500.00 and up.

This large mocha-decorated pitcher spells out "ALE" in slip dots on a strong brown slip band. The barrel shape is an early English form and is circa 1810. Other similarly decorated pitchers have been found with different names. $3,500.00 and up.

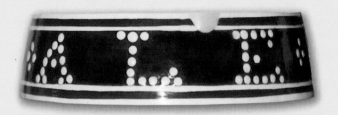

This is the ultimate Swan Hill pitcher: a hound handle, a big frog inside, a presentation name, and a great Rockingham and cobalt glaze. The vine and grapes design molded on the body of the pitcher is different from the usual hunt scene. The presentation name, "J.C. TOUNSEND," is done in scrolled letters instead of the typical block letters. It is lower on the body due to the massive spout. New Jersey, circa 1865. 10" tall. $4,000.00 and up.

A wide slip band is an unusual addition to this transfer-decorated pitcher. There is a different parrot transfer on each side. England, circa 1840. 6" high. $550.00 – 750.00.

A rarely seen covered pitcher, the work of Charles Coxon when he worked in Baltimore, Maryland, for the E. & W. Bennett pottery. The spout, which is pierced, has a goat's head molded on it. The design on the body is herons, one of which is attacking a snake curled around the handle. Fortunately the Rockingham glaze does not obscure the incredible detail. The design was copied in Canada but lacks the quality of this pitcher. 10" high. $1,200.00 and up.

Strictly a nineteenth century production, batter bowls, or lipped bowls, as they were called on potters' bills of sale, can be difficult to find. The most commonly seen batter bowls are embossed. Two styles were made at the Jeffords pottery in Philadelphia, Pennslyvania and by D.E. McNicol in East Liverpool, Ohio. The Jeffords version (Book 1, Plate 34c) is more ornate; the McNicol batter bowl (a Rockingham example, Book 1, Plate 34a) has a vertical, pointed design with scalloped rim. The Croxall batter bowl (shown in this chapter) is simplest. There are other embossed designs from England and Canada. Sizes range from about 7" in diameter to about 16", but not in all designs.

Banded and mocha-decorated batter bowls were not made in sets. The sizes for them range from about 9" to 14" in diameter. It may be possible to build a group of three or four similar ones in graduated sizes, if you know an active dealer and have patience! This type of batter bowl was produced in England and the United States.

This embossed pattern was produced at the Croxall and C. C. Thompson potteries in at least four sizes. This example is 15¾" in diameter, the largest size found. 1860 – 1890. $295.00 – 495.00, depending on diameter.

This is the simplest mocha decoration found on batter bowls. Blue seaweed examples may or may not have a rolled rim. The rolled rim is later than the plain rim. 1850 – 1890. $850.00 and up, depending on size.

Banded batter bowls, United States and England. 1850 – 1880. $850.00 and up, each, depending on diameter and quality of bands (amount, number of colors).

Marked "PACIFIC" mixing bowl with floral copper lustre decoration, California, 1920 – 1930, 9" diameter. $350.00 – 450.00.

Blue seaweed looks like an afterthought on this banded bowl. The slip bands, although plentiful, are not skillfully done. Baltimore, Maryland, or East Liverpool, Ohio, circa 1870. 13" diameter. $550.00 – 795.00.

A rare occasion where yellow ware was substituted for stoneware. This Diamond and Currants pattern bowl is usually found as blue and white stoneware. Ohio, circa 1900. $350.00 – 450.00.

The Brighton Pottery Co., Zanesville, Ohio, only used this mark for two years. (To see this mark, go to Book 2, Potters & Their Marks.) They were the only pottery to use this combination of color and technique for decoration. 6" diameter. $395.00 – 495.00.

This plain yellow bowl has an interesting, shallow embossed design. England or Canada. 12" diameter, circa 1900. $125.00 – 195.00.

The National Pottery impressed their utilitarian pieces with "NATIONAL," and the head of an Indian in full headdress. The company was in Roseville, Ohio and in business circa 1920 – 1940. The bowl shown is about 4" in diameter and glazed only on the inside, for practical purposes. $100.00 – 150.00.

The mocha decoration on this bowl does not have a name. The potter applied slip bands in brown and white and then, skillfully manipulated them with a tool. The effect is similar to a ragged wall. A unique piece at this time. Ohio, nineteenth century. $1,800.00 and up.

The twentieth century banded bowl was the most common piece of yellow ware produced. These bowls were produced in huge quantities, especially from the 1920s through the 1940s. Most bowls were part of a kitchenware line, and matching pitchers, crocks, custard cups, etc., can sometimes be found. The earliest bowls, those from 1850 – 1860, are either embossed or white banded. The white bands are generally wide bands, although there were some bowls with multiple narrow white bands as well. Bowls were not the bulk of the production for yellowware potteries in the nineteenth century. Some potteries did not make bowls at all. Nappies, however, were widely made.

J.E. Jeffords in Philadelphia seems to have made quite a few bowls compared to his peers. Most of the best banded bowls, the ones with a dozen or more bands in one or more colors, can be firmly attributed to Jeffords. Blue, brown, and white were the only colors used for slip bands in this time period. Jeffords made the bulk of the banded colanders that are found; it was a short step to pierce the bowl and produce a colander. The Jeffords bowls date from circa 1870. The early Morton, Illinois, pottery Morton Pottery Works, opening in 1878, produced a bowl with four narrow white rings and a cross-hatched embossed pattern below the bands. Syracuse Stoneware Co. in New York made brown and white banded bowls in the late 1800s, as did C.C. Thompson in East Liverpool, Ohio. By this time production of bowls had stepped up.

One of the earliest attributable bowls of the twentieth century is part of the Dandy Line. Brush McCoy produced this kitchenware line starting in 1915. The bowls of this line have white bands, which, along with the thick, primitive clay, confuse collectors into thinking that they are nineteenth century. There are two band patterns in this line. The first is a wide band encompassed by a single narrow band on each side. The second pattern is three narrow bands. Later, a wide range of colors was used in banding bowls. Army green, various pinks, and black were among the colors used in addition to the standard blues, browns, and white. Bowls that were embossed as well as banded were common, although the embossing was much sharper than in the nineteenth century. Another twentieth century characteristic was the change in rim, from none or rolled to extended and squared off. This rim offered more space for decoration, whether embossing or slip bands, because of its flat surface. A general change in the composition of the clay from mostly yellowware to mostly or all stoneware was signaled by the use of the flat rim.

The composition of the body is a factor in dating bowls as well. Although stoneware has been mixed with yellow ware since circa 1869, earlier pieces are predominately yellow earthenware. By the 1930s, the yellow appearance of mixing bowls was less yellow and/or flecked because the body was mostly (or all) stoneware. This was a boon for the homemaker and the pottery; the bowls were much sturdier, lasted longer, and the pottery had fewer complaints. The last resort for the potteries was a stoneware bowl with a bright yellow glaze to imitate yellow ware. If you want to collect yellow pieces for decorative purposes these are fine, but you are no longer collecting yellow ware at this point.

Yellow ware bowls from the twentieth century are where many collectors begin. They are plentiful, and you see them everywhere; television programs and commercials, magazines, movies. Also, many collectors think that they have to start out "small." As an experienced dealer, I've found that this can be a mistake, for a few reasons. The first reason is that, at some point, you will want to "trade up," and if you start buying unusual pieces from the beginning, this trading up point will never come. Along with this, you can get a strong start before prices rise. With the current spike in the prices of some twentieth century yellow ware bowls, you can get some truly unusual nineteenth century pieces for the same price as a 1930s bowl (due in part to auctions, some recent prices for these bowls are over-inflated). You will learn more about yellow ware from owning a nineteenth century piece than from most twentieth century pieces. These later bowls are your choice to collect, but caution should be paid to price and condition.

When it is possible, I have listed the maker and sizes made with each bowl. When a bowl is not marked or if it has not been found on a pottery's bill of sale, it can be impossible to attribute it. Potteries in Zanesville, Ohio, and the surrounding area, Fultonham, Roseville, and Crooksville, produced many of these bowls post-1920. Unless a catalog or bill of sale is available, the range of sizes made will also be impossible to state. Pfaltzgraff is the only pottery known to have produced a bowl in every size, from 4" to 18" in diameter. Along with a range of prices (the high end being for the largest examples), I have put a price range on a 9" – 10" bowl, since this is an average size and the easiest to find. Although every twentieth century banded bowl made is not represented here, there is a good cross-section shown.

An obviously popular form, this page shows five band patterns, in order of rarity: blue and white, pink and blue, green and white, black and white, and pink and brown. Known sizes: 4½"–12". $85.00 – 325.00 , depending on color combination and size. 9-10" bowl, $95.00 – 175.00, depending on color.

Left, Morton Pottery, Morton, IL., after 1922. The red band is over-glaze. 5" diameter. $75.00 – 110.00. Right, 11", unusual light and dark blue bands, $150.00 – 185.00.

Watt Pottery, Crooksville, Ohio, 1955 – 1965. Yellow stoneware called Kitch-N-Queen. 10" diameter. $25.00 – 35.00.

Weller Pottery. (See Potters' Marks.) Unusual olive green bands. 8" diameter. $100.00 – 135.00.

This embossed design of a girl watering flowers is probably McCoy, since they used "U.S.A." as a mark. 5" – 10" diameter. $100.00 – 175.00 , depending on size. 9" – 10" bowl, $135.00 – 175.00.

Chocolate and white bands, 5¼" to 11½" in diameter. There is a lot of stoneware in this bowl. The large number of bands elevates the price. $100.00 – 225.00, depending on size. 9" – 10" bowl, $100.00 – 125.00.

Plain yellow ware 4" bowl with a clear glaze. $85.00 – 125.00.

The bowl with four bands is Morton Pottery Company, 1922 to at least 1929. Five bowls were made, from 5" to 9" according to the catalog, but bowls up to 11" are known. $100.00 – 225.00, depending on size. The bowl with five bands is probably also Morton (note the identical form even though the clay is a different color). The bowls with three bands are Brush McCoy, from 1915 to 1925. (Note lack of shoulder rim in comparison to Morton bowls.) 4½" and 5" to 12". $95.00 – 275.00, depending on size. 9-10" bowl, $100.00 – 140.00.

Weller Pottery (see Potters' Marks). Sizes are about 5" to 12". Brown-banded bowls are less expensive due to general lack of popularity. Bowl shown is 6". $65.00 – 200.00, depending on size. 9" – 10" bowl, $75.00 – 100.00.

Watt Pottery, Crooksville, Ohio, circa 1930s. I have seen these with a wide blue band as well as brown. 9" bowl shown. $65.00 – 95.00.

Stoneware bowl with brown and blue bands, pale yellow clay, marked with a crown. This mark is attributed to Robinson Ransbottom Pottery Company, Roseville, Ohio, because of the composition of the clay. This mark was used from 1935 to ?, 10" bowl shown. $95.00 – 125.00.

9" bowl with brown bands and embossed flowers. The embossed decoration elevates the price of this brown banded bowl. $85.00 – 125.00.

Hull Pottery Company, Crooksville, Ohio. Marked with the "H" in a circle, which was used from 1910 to 1935. 9 – 10" bowl (shown), $75.00 – 100.00.

12" embossed bowl with blue bands. $150.00 – 195.00.

5" embossed bowl with brown bands. $85.00 – 125.00.

Pfaltzgraff, York, Pennsylvania, produced this band pattern circa 1920 – 1930. The bowl with three white bands was experimental. 4" to 18". $100.00 – 500.00, depending on size; 9-10" bowl, $100.00 – 125.00.

Blue-banded bowl with concave "pillows." Possibly Hull Pottery, Crooksville, Ohio, 1930s. 8" bowl shown, $75.00 – 95.00.

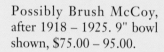

Possibly Brush McCoy, after 1918 – 1925. 9" bowl shown, $75.00 – 95.00.

Possibly Weller, due to the form, band pattern, and unglazed bottom. 9" bowl shown, $100.00 – 150.00.

These bowls were produced by the Nelson McCoy pottery in Roseville, Ohio. The pottery started in 1910, but the characteristics of this type of bowl date it to after 1935. 4½" to 11¾". $75.00 – 175.00, depending on size. 9-10" bowl, 75.00 – 100.00.

Yellow ware with this band pattern is from a kitchenware line called "Zane Grey." It was produced by the Hull Pottery, Crooksville, Ohio, circa 1930s. It was also produced with brown bands instead of navy blue bands. 4⅛" to 15¼". $75.00 – 400.00, depending on size. 9-10" bowl, $85.00 – 110.00.

Embossed brown and white banded bowl with hexagonal base. 9" bowl shown, $80.00 – 100.00.

Embossed blue and white banded bowl. 10" bowl shown, $80.00 –100.00.

Pink and white banded embossed bowl. 5" bowl shown, $95.00 –135.00.

Green-glazed bowls date 1920s – 1940s and were made by many Ohio potteries. Most of these bowls are not yellow ware, but stoneware. The Nelson McCoy Pottery, Roseville, Ohio, made square bottomed green-glazed bowls with a variety of embossed patterns. Sizes are approximately 5" to 11" in diameter. $65.00 – 125.00, depending on size. 9" – 10" bowl, $65.00 – 100.00.

Rare set of green-glazed bowls with girl watering flowers, 5" – 9".

Nelson McCoy bowl.

Selected Bibliography

Barrett, Richard Carter. *Bennington Pottery and Porcelain: A Guide to Identification*. New York: Crown Publishers, Inc., 1958.

Branin, Lelyn M. *The Early Makers of Handcrafted Earthenware and Stoneware in Central and Southern New Jersey*, New Jersey: Associated University Presses, Inc., 1988.

Cruickshank, Graeme. *Scottish Pottery*, Shire Publications Ltd., Aylesbury, Bucks, UK. 1987.

Fitzgerald, Glenna G. *Molds*, February 18, 1991.

Gallo, John. *Nineteenth and Twentieth Century Yellow Ware*. New York: Heritage Press, 1985.

Godden, Geoffrey A. *Encyclopedia of British Pottery and Porcelain Marks*. New York: F.R.S.A. Bonanza Books, MCMLXIV.

Hall, Doris and Burdell. *Morton's Potteries: 99 Years*. Nixa, MO: A and J Printers, 1982.

Huxford, Sharon and Bob. *The Collectors Encyclopedia of McCoy Pottery*, Collector Books, 1980.

Jersey City: Shaping America's Pottery Industry 1825 – 1892, exhibition at Jersey City Museum, Jersey City, New Jersey. 1997.

Katz-Marks, Mariann. *The Collector's Encyclopedia of Majolica*. Collector Books, 1992.

Ketchum, William C. , Jr., *Potters and Potteries of New York State, 1650 - 1900*, Second Edition, Syracuse University Press, 1987.

Lehner, Lois. *Lehner's Encyclopedia of U.S. Marks on Pottery, Porcelain, and Clay*. Paducah, KY: Collector Books, 1988.

Leibowitz, Joan. *Yellow Ware: The Transitional Ceramic*. Exton, PA: Schiffer Publishing, 1985.

Lewis, John and Griselda. *Prattware English and Scottish Relief Decorated and Underglaze Colored Earthenware 1780 – 1840*. Antique Collector's Club, 1984.

McAllister, Lisa S. and John L. Michel. *Collecting Yellow Ware*. Paducah, KY: Collector Books, 1993.

McNeill, Carol. *Kirkcaldy Potteries*, Fife Publicity, 1998.

McNerney, Kathryn. *Blue and White Stoneware: An Identification and Value Guide*. Paducah, KY: Collector Books, 1981.

Morris, Sue and Dave. *Watt Pottery, An Identification and Value Guide*, Collector Books, 1998.

Rickard, Jonathan. The Makers of Dip't, Banded, Colour'd and Mocha wares, Brandywine River Museum of the Brandywine Conservancy, 1995, printed by Pearl Pressman Liberty, Philadelphia, PA.

Roberts, Brenda. *The Collector's Encyclopedia of Hull Pottery*. Paducah, KY: Collector Books, 1980.

Sanford, Martha and Steve. *The Guide to Brush-McCoy Pottery*. Clarksville, TN: Jostens, Inc., 1992.

Stradling, J.G. "Puzzling aspects of the most popular piece of American pottery ever made," *The Magazine Antiques*, February 1997.

Stradling, Diana and J. G. "The Jacqueline D. Hodgson Collection of Important American Ceramics," Sotheby Parke Bernet Inc., January 1974.

DOLLS, FIGURES & TEDDY BEARS

4631	**Barbie Doll** Boom, 1986–1995, Augustyniak	$18.95
2079	**Barbie Doll** Fashion, Volume I, Eames	$24.95
4846	**Barbie Doll** Fashion, Volume II, Eames	$24.95
3957	**Barbie** Exclusives, Rana	$18.95
4632	**Barbie** Exclusives, Book II, Rana	$18.95
6022	The **Barbie Doll** Years, 5th Ed., Olds	$19.95
3810	**Chatty Cathy** Dolls, Lewis	$15.95
5352	Collector's Ency. of **Barbie** Doll Exclusives & More, 2nd Ed., Augustyniak	$24.95
4863	Collector's Encyclopedia of **Vogue Dolls**, Izen/Stover	$29.95
5904	Collector's Guide to **Celebrity Dolls**, Spurgeon	$24.95
5599	Collector's Guide to **Dolls of the 1960s and 1970s**, Sabulis	$24.95
6030	Collector's Guide to **Horsman Dolls**, Jensen	$29.95
6025	**Doll Values**, Antique to Modern, 6th Ed., Moyer	$12.95
6033	**Modern Collectible Dolls**, Volume VI, Moyer	$24.95
5689	**Nippon Dolls** & Playthings, Van Patten/Lau	$29.95
5365	**Peanuts** Collectibles, Podley/Bang	$24.95
6026	**Small Dolls of the 40s & 50s**, Stover	$29.95
5253	Story of **Barbie**, 2nd Ed., Westenhouser	$24.95
5277	**Talking Toys** of the 20th Century, Lewis	$15.95
2084	**Teddy Bears, Annalee's & Steiff** Animals, 3rd Series, Mandel	$19.95
1808	Wonder of **Barbie**, Manos	$9.95
1430	World of **Barbie** Dolls, Manos	$9.95
4880	World of **Raggedy Ann** Collectibles, Avery	$24.95

TOYS & MARBLES

2333	Antique & Collectible **Marbles**, 3rd Ed., Grist	$9.95
4559	Collectible **Action Figures**, 2nd Ed., Manos	$17.95
5900	Collector's Guide to **Battery Toys**, 2nd Edition, Hultzman	$24.95
4566	Collector's Guide to **Tootsietoys**, 2nd Ed., Richter	$19.95
5169	Collector's Guide to **TV Toys** & Memorabilia, 2nd Ed., Davis/Morgan	$24.95
5593	Grist's Big Book of **Marbles**, 2nd Ed.	$24.95
3970	Grist's Machine-Made & Contemporary **Marbles**, 2nd Ed.	$9.95
5267	**Matchbox Toys**, 1947 to 1998, 3rd Ed., Johnson	$19.95
5830	**McDonald's** Collectibles, 2nd Edition, Henriques/DuVall	$24.95
5673	Modern **Candy Containers** & Novelties, Brush/Miller	$19.95
1540	Modern **Toys** 1930–1980, Baker	$19.95
5920	**Schroeder's Collectible Toys**, Antique to Modern Price Guide, 8th Ed.	$17.95
5908	**Toy Car** Collector's Guide, Johnson	$19.95

FURNITURE

3716	American **Oak** Furniture, Book II, McNerney	$12.95
1118	Antique **Oak** Furniture, Hill	$7.95
3720	Collector's Encyclopedia of **American** Furniture, Vol. III, Swedberg	$24.95
5359	Early **American** Furniture, Obbard	$12.95
3906	**Heywood-Wakefield** Modern Furniture, Rouland	$18.95
1885	**Victorian** Furniture, Our American Heritage, McNerney	$9.95
3829	**Victorian** Furniture, Our American Heritage, Book II, McNerney	$9.95

JEWELRY, HATPINS, WATCHES & PURSES

4704	Antique & Collectible **Buttons**, Wisniewski	$19.95
1748	Antique **Purses**, Revised Second Ed., Holiner	$19.95
4850	Collectible **Costume Jewelry**, Simonds	$24.95
5675	Collectible **Silver Jewelry**, Rezazadeh	$24.95
	Collector's Ency. of **Compacts**, Carryalls & Face Powder Boxes, Mueller	$24.95
	...me Jewelry, A Practical Handbook & Value Guide, Rezazadeh	$24.95
	...ears of Collectible **Fashion Jewelry**, 1925–1975, Baker	$24.95

1424	**Hatpins** & Hatpin Holders, Baker	$9.95
5695	**Ladies' Vintage Accessories**, Bruton	$24.95
1181	100 Years of Collectible **Jewelry**, 1850–1950, Baker	$9.95
4729	**Sewing Tools** & Trinkets, Thompson	$24.95
6038	**Sewing Tools** & Trinkets, Volume 2, Thompson	$24.95
6039	Signed Beauties of **Costume Jewelry**, Brown	$24.95
5620	Unsigned Beauties of **Costume Jewelry**, Brown	$24.95
4878	Vintage & Contemporary **Purse Accessories**, Gerson	$24.95
5696	Vintage & Vogue Ladies' **Compacts**, 2nd Edition, Gerson	$29.95
5923	**Vintage Jewelry** for Investment & Casual Wear, Edeen	$24.95

INDIANS, GUNS, KNIVES, TOOLS, PRIMITIVES

6021	**Arrowheads** of the Central Great Plains, Fox	$19.95
1868	Antique **Tools**, Our American Heritage, McNerney	$9.95
5616	Big Book of **Pocket Knives**, Stewart	$19.95
4943	Field Guide to Flint **Arrowheads** & Knives of the North American Indian	$9.95
3885	**Indian Artifacts** of the Midwest, Book II, Hothem	$16.95
4870	**Indian Artifacts** of the Midwest, Book III, Hothem	$18.95
5685	**Indian Artifacts** of the Midwest, Book IV, Hothem	$19.95
6132	**Modern Guns**, Identification & Values, 14th Ed., Quertermous	$14.95
2164	**Primitives**, Our American Heritage, McNerney	$9.95
1759	**Primitives**, Our American Heritage, 2nd Series, McNerney	$14.95
6031	Standard **Knife** Collector's Guide, 4th Ed., Ritchie & Stewart	$14.95
5999	**Wilderness** Survivor's Guide, Hamper	$12.95

PAPER COLLECTIBLES & BOOKS

4633	Big Little Books, Jacobs	$18.95
5902	**Boys' & Girls' Book** Series	$19.95
4710	Collector's Guide to **Children's Books**, 1850 to 1950, Volume I, Jones	$18.95
5153	Collector's Guide to **Children's Books**, 1850 to 1950, Volume II, Jones	$19.95
1441	Collector's Guide to **Post Cards**, Wood	$9.95
5926	**Duck Stamps**, Chappell	$9.95
2081	Guide to Collecting **Cookbooks**, Allen	$14.95
2080	Price Guide to **Cookbooks** & Recipe Leaflets, Dickinson	$9.95
3973	**Sheet Music** Reference & Price Guide, 2nd Ed., Pafik & Guiheen	$19.95
6041	Vintage **Postcards** for the Holidays, Reed	$24.95
4733	**Whitman Juvenile Books**, Brown	$17.95

GLASSWARE

5602	Anchor Hocking's **Fire-King** & More, 2nd Ed.	$24.95
5823	Collectible **Glass Shoes**, 2nd Edition, Wheatley	$24.95
5897	Coll. **Glassware** from the 40s, 50s & 60s, 6th Ed., Florence	$19.95
1810	Collector's Encyclopedia of **American Art Glass**, Shuman	$29.95
5907	Collector's Encyclopedia of **Depression Glass**, 15th Ed., Florence	$19.95
1961	Collector's Encyclopedia of **Fry Glassware**, Fry Glass Society	$24.95
1664	Collector's Encyclopedia of **Heisey Glass**, 1925–1938, Bredehoft	$24.95
3905	Collector's Encyclopedia of **Milk Glass**, Newbound	$24.95
4936	Collector's Guide to **Candy Containers**, Dezso/Poirier	$19.95
5820	Collector's Guide to **Glass Banks**, Reynolds	$24.95
4564	**Crackle Glass**, Weitman	$19.95
4941	**Crackle Glass**, Book II, Weitman	$19.95
4714	**Czechoslovakian Glass** and Collectibles, Book II, Barta/Rose	$16.95
5528	Early American **Pattern Glass**, Metz	$17.95
6125	**Elegant Glassware** of the Depression Era, 10th Ed., Florence	$24.95
3981	Evers' Standard **Cut Glass** Value Guide	$12.95
5614	Field Guide to **Pattern Glass**, McCain	$17.95
5615	Florence's **Glassware Pattern Identification** Guide, Vol. II	$19.95

9	**Fostoria**, Etched, Carved & Cut Designs, Vol. II, Kerr	$24.95
1	**Fostoria Tableware**, 1924 – 1943, Long/Seate	$24.95
1	**Fostoria Tableware**, 1944 – 1986, Long/Seate	$24.95
4	**Fostoria**, Useful & Ornamental, Long/Seate	$29.95
9	**Glass & Ceramic Baskets**, White	$19.95
4	**Imperial Carnival Glass**, Burns	$18.95
7	**Kitchen Glassware** of the Depression Years, 6th Ed., Florence	$24.95
0	Much More Early American **Pattern Glass**, Metz	$17.95
5	**Northwood Carnival Glass**, 1908 – 1925, Burns	$19.95
6	Pocket Guide to **Depression Glass**, 13th Ed., Florence	$12.95
3	Standard Encyclopedia of **Carnival Glass**, 8th Ed., Edwards/Carwile	$29.95
4	Standard **Carnival Glass** Price Guide, 13th Ed., Edwards/Carwile	$9.95
5	Standard Encyclopedia of **Opalescent Glass**, 4th Ed., Edwards/Carwile	$24.95
2	**Very Rare Glassware** of the Depression Years, 5th Series, Florence	$24.95

POTTERY

7	**ABC Plates & Mugs**, Lindsay	$24.95
9	**American Art Pottery**, Sigafoose	$24.95
0	**American Limoges**, Limoges	$24.95
2	**Blue & White Stoneware**, McNerney	$9.95
9	**Blue Willow**, 2nd Ed., Gaston	$14.95
1	Collectible **Cups & Saucers**, Harran	$18.95
3	Collector's Encyclopedia of **American Dinnerware**, Cunningham	$24.95
1	Collector's Encyclopedia of **Bauer Pottery**, Chipman	$24.95
4	Collector's Encyclopedia of **California Pottery**, 2nd Ed., Chipman	$24.95
3	Collector's Encyclopedia of **Cookie Jars**, Book II, Roerig	$24.95
9	Collector's Encyclopedia of **Cookie Jars**, Book III, Roerig	$24.95
8	Collector's Encyclopedia of **Fiesta**, 9th Ed., Huxford	$24.95
1	Collector's Encyclopedia of **Early Noritake**, Alden	$24.95
2	Collector's Encyclopedia of **Flow Blue China**, 2nd Ed., Gaston	$24.95
1	Collector's Encyclopedia of **Homer Laughlin China**, Jasper	$24.95
6	Collector's Encyclopedia of **Hull Pottery**, Roberts	$19.95
2	Collector's Encyclopedia of **Lefton China**, DeLozier	$19.95
5	Collector's Encyclopedia of **Lefton China**, Book II, DeLozier	$19.95
9	Collector's Encyclopedia of **Limoges Porcelain**, 3rd Ed., Gaston	$29.95
4	Collector's Encyclopedia of **Majolica Pottery**, Katz-Marks	$19.95
8	Collector's Encyclopedia of **McCoy Pottery**, Huxford	$19.95
7	Collector's Encyclopedia of **Niloak**, 2nd Edition, Gifford	$29.95
7	Collector's Encyclopedia of **Nippon Porcelain**, Van Patten	$24.95
5	Collector's Ency. of **Nippon Porcelain**, 3rd Series, Van Patten	$24.95
3	Collector's Ency. of **Nippon Porcelain**, 5th Series, Van Patten	$24.95
7	Collector's Ency. of **Nippon Porcelain**, 6th Series, Van Patten	$29.95
7	Collector's Encyclopedia of **Noritake**, Van Patten	$19.95
4	Collector's Encyclopedia of **Pickard China**, Reed	$29.95
9	Collector's Encyclopedia of **Red Wing Art Pottery**, Dollen	$24.95
8	Collector's Encyclopedia of **Rosemeade Pottery**, Dommel	$24.95
1	Collector's Encyclopedia of **Roseville Pottery**, Revised, Huxford/Nickel	$24.95
2	Collector's Encyclopedia of **Roseville Pottery**, 2nd Series, Huxford/Nickel	$24.95
7	Collector's Encyclopedia of **Russel Wright**, 3rd Editon, Kerr	$29.95
0	Collector's Encyclopedia of **Stangl Dinnerware**, Runge	$24.95
1	Collector's Encyclopedia of **Stangl Artware**, Lamps, and Birds, Runge	$29.95
4	Collector's Encyclopedia of **Van Briggle Art Pottery**, Sasicki	$24.95
0	Collector's Guide to **Feather Edge Ware**, McAllister	$19.95
6	Collector's Guide to **Lu-Ray Pastels**, Meehan	$18.95
4	Collector's Guide to **Made in Japan Ceramics**, White	$18.95
6	Collector's Guide to **Made in Japan Ceramics**, Book II, White	$18.95
5	**Cookie Jars**, Westfall	$9.95
0	**Cookie Jars**, Book II, Westfall	$19.95
9	**Dresden Porcelain** Studios, Harran	$29.95
8	Florence's Big Book of **Salt & Pepper Shakers**	$24.95

2379	Lehner's Ency. of **U.S. Marks** on Pottery, Porcelain & China	$24.95
4722	**McCoy Pottery**, Collector's Reference & Value Guide, Hanson/Nissen	$19.95
5913	**McCoy Pottery**, Volume III, Hanson & Nissen	$24.95
5691	**Post86 Fiesta**, Identification & Value Guide, Racheter	$19.95
1670	**Red Wing Collectibles**, DePasquale	$9.95
1440	**Red Wing Stoneware**, DePasquale	$9.95
6037	**Rookwood Pottery**, Nicholson & Thomas	$24.95
1632	**Salt & Pepper Shakers**, Guarnaccia	$9.95
5091	**Salt & Pepper Shakers** II, Guarnaccia	$18.95
3443	**Salt & Pepper Shakers** IV, Guarnaccia	$18.95
3738	**Shawnee Pottery**, Mangus	$24.95
4629	Turn of the Century **American Dinnerware**, 1880s–1920s, Jasper	$24.95
3327	**Watt Pottery** – Identification & Value Guide, Morris	$19.95
5924	**Zanesville Stoneware** Company, Rans, Ralston & Russell	$24.95

OTHER COLLECTIBLES

5916	Advertising **Paperweights**, Holiner & Kammerman	$24.95
5838	Advertising **Thermometers**, Merritt	$16.95
5898	Antique & Contemporary **Advertising Memorabilia**, Summers	$24.95
5814	Antique **Brass & Copper** Collectibles, Gaston	$24.95
1880	Antique **Iron**, McNerney	$9.95
3872	Antique **Tins**, Dodge	$24.95
4845	Antique **Typewriters & Office Collectibles**, Rehr	$19.95
5607	Antiquing and Collecting on the **Internet**, Parry	$12.95
1128	**Bottle** Pricing Guide, 3rd Ed., Cleveland	$7.95
3718	Collectible **Aluminum**, Grist	$16.95
5060	Collectible **Souvenir Spoons**, Bednersh	$19.95
5676	Collectible **Souvenir Spoons**, Book II, Bednersh	$29.95
5666	Collector's Encyclopedia of **Granite Ware**, Book 2, Greguire	$29.95
5836	Collector's Guide to **Antique Radios**, 5th Ed., Bunis	$19.95
3966	Collector's Guide to **Inkwells**, Identification & Values, Badders	$18.95
4947	Collector's Guide to **Inkwells**, Book II, Badders	$19.95
5681	Collector's Guide to **Lunchboxes**, White	$19.95
5621	Collector's Guide to **Online Auctions**, Hix	$12.95
4864	Collector's Guide to **Wallace Nutting Pictures**, Ivankovich	$18.95
5683	**Fishing Lure** Collectibles, Vol. 1, Murphy/Edmisten	$29.95
5911	**Flea Market Trader**, 13th Ed., Huxford	$9.95
6227	**Garage Sale** & Flea Market Annual, 11th Edition, Huxford	$19.95
4945	**G-Men and FBI Toys** and Collectibles, Whitworth	$18.95
3819	**General Store** Collectibles, Wilson	$24.95
5912	The **Heddon Legacy**, A Century of Classic Lures, Roberts & Pavey	$29.95
2216	**Kitchen Antiques**, 1790–1940, McNerney	$14.95
5991	**Lighting Devices** & Accessories of the 17th – 19th Centuries, Hamper	$9.95
5686	**Lighting Fixtures** of the Depression Era, Book I, Thomas	$24.95
4950	The **Lone Ranger**, Collector's Reference & Value Guide, Felbinger	$18.95
6028	Modern **Fishing Lure** Collectibles, Vol. 1, Lewis	$24.95
6131	Modern **Fishing Lure** Collectibles, Vol. 2, Lewis	$24.95
2026	**Railroad** Collectibles, 4th Ed., Baker	$14.95
5619	**Roy Rogers and Dale Evans** Toys & Memorabilia, Coyle	$24.95
6137	**Schroeder's Antiques** Price Guide, 21st Edition	$14.95
5007	**Silverplated Flatware**, Revised 4th Edition, Hagan	$18.95
6239	**Star Wars** Super Collector's Wish Book, 2nd Ed., Carlton	$29.95
6139	Summers' Guide to **Coca-Cola**, 4th Ed.	$24.95
5905	Summers' Pocket Guide to **Coca-Cola**, 3rd Ed.	$12.95
3977	Value Guide to **Gas Station Memorabilia**, Summers & Priddy	$24.95
4877	Vintage **Bar Ware**, Visakay	$24.95
5925	The Vintage Era of **Golf Club Collectibles**, John	$29.95
6010	The Vintage Era of **Golf Club Collectibles** Collector's Log, John	$9.95
6036	Vintage **Quilts**, Aug, Newman & Roy	$24.95
4935	The W.F. Cody **Buffalo Bill** Collector's Guide with Values	$24.95

This is only a partial listing of the books on antiques that are available from Collector Books. All books are well illustrated and contain current values. Most of these books are available from your local bookseller, antique dealer, or public library. If you are unable to locate certain titles in your area, you may order by mail from **COLLECTOR BOOKS**, P.O. Box 3009, Paducah, KY 42002-3009. Customers with Visa, Master Card, or Discover may phone in orders from 8:00–5:00 CST, Monday–Friday, Toll Free **1-800-626-5420**, or online at **www.collectorbooks.com**. Add $3.00 for postage for the first book ordered and 50¢ for each additional book. Include item number, title, and price when ordering. Allow 14 to 21 days for delivery.

1-800-626-5420 Fax: 1-270-898-8890

www.collectorbooks.com

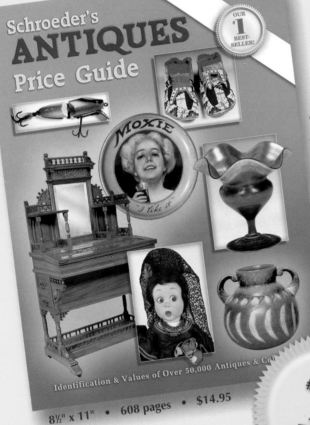